NOW IT'S OUR TURN

How Women Can Transform
Their Lives and Save the Planet

NOW IT'S OUR TURN

How Women Can Transform Their Lives and Save the Planet

ALANA LYONS

**JAGUAR
BOOKS** INC

Published by Jaguar Books, Inc.
23852 Pacific Coast Hwy., Ste. 756
Malibu, CA 90265

Editor: Nancy Grimley Carleton
Editorial Assistant: Claudette Charbonneau
Cover Art: Jim Warren
Cover Design: Lightbourne Images
Book Design and Composition: Classic Typography

Manufactured in the United States of America.

*Printed on Halopaque Antique, a blend
of recycled and postconsumer paper.*

10 9 8 7 6 5 4 3 2 1

Library of Congress Cataloging-in-Publication Data

Lyons, Alana.
    Now it's our turn : how women can transform their lives and save
the planet / Alana Lyons.
        p.   cm.
    Includes bibliographical references and index.
    ISBN 0-9663694-0-8
    1. Ecofeminism.   2. Nature—Effect of human beings on.   3. Women—
Psychology.   4. Women—Religious life.   5. New age movement.
I. Title.
HQ1233.L96   1998
305.42   dc21
                                                                98-26346
                                                                    CIP

This book is dedicated
to my mother and grandmother,
who were ahead of their time.

And thank you to my two older half-sisters, who created the
experience for me to have to learn to take my power alone and
who gave me the desire to want to bring women together.

Many of the teachings which inspired the author
and which you find in this book were taught
by shaman and Elder Thunder Strikes.

Contents

Contents

Part Three: The Reality of Our Lives in the Workplace

Part Four: Our Place in Our World

Preface

I have written *Now It's Our Turn* with the hope that it will inspire you to take a multifaceted look at all aspects of your life, from your personal relationships with men and other family members, to your position in the workplace, to your connection with Mother Earth and your crucial role in healing the current threats to life on our beloved planet.

To create change, whether in our personal lives or in the world at large, we first have to understand the problems and challenges we face. We have to see clearly. We have to wake up to the reality of what is happening to us and our planet. In this book I have balanced Awakening chapters, which clearly describe the existing challenges and inequities we face, with Solutions chapters, which stress positive, practical, and spiritual steps we can take to reclaim and integrate our feminine power and make the changes we desire. You may find some of the information in the Awakening chapters disquieting, even painful, for much damage has been done both to women and to our planet by centuries of male domination. If you find some of this information overwhelming, take it in small doses, but remember that hope and inspiration will follow as you explore the powerful ideas in the Solutions chapters. So have faith: There is hope, and together we can create the changes to solve even the most seemingly insurmountable problems we face, both personally and collectively.

Now It's Our Turn serves as a guidebook for creating gender balance both in your private life and in your life in the world. After several millennia during which humanity's history and daily affairs have largely been controlled by the energies and values of men, now it's your turn, as a woman, to play a key role in restoring the balance of feminine energies on the planet. In the process, your personal life will be enriched immeasurably.

As you read *Now It's Our Turn* and work with the ideas and suggestions here, you will find your life changing in positive ways you have only dreamed of. Your relationships and your home life can become infinitely more satisfying. You can learn to empower yourself more fully in the workplace. And finally, you can answer the call for us to come forth as women and claim the mantle of authority to help save life on Earth. You were born into this time for a purpose! Please join with me, in this, the most important mission of our time.

Alana Lyons
Malibu, California

Acknowledgments

How can I begin to acknowledge the people who have made such a difference in my life? Simply saying "thank you" seems so trite for those who have helped me in achieving my sacred dream. Nevertheless, I extend a loving thank you to my husband, who dreamed the title for the book, *Now It's Our Turn,* in his sleep one night, and who deserves my deepest gratitude for the support he gave me during all the nights I spent writing and researching instead of with him.

I also wish to thank Twisted Hair Elder Thunder Strikes, whose teachings and open sharing of many truths are reflected throughout this book. He has helped shed light on how critical the balance of masculine and feminine energies is in all living things in creation.

Many thanks to the women friends in my life who have given me the courage and support to follow my sacred dream. Without their energy and encouragement, I might have faltered. I especially wish to thank Janene Behl, Jan Morris, who sent me every research article she could find, and Janice Holmes, who helped me to rewrite and reorganize the exercises and make corrections throughout this book.

A special note of thanks and appreciation to Nancy Grimley Carleton, my friend and editor. I am more of an idea person with a passion than I am a writer. Nancy took my ideas and put them into a more organized and developed form. She gave me encouragement at moments when I was ready to give up, and helped bring the project to completion. The assistance of Claudette Charbonneau in providing up-to-date references was also most valuable.

Geraldine Hatch-Hannon helped me with my work from the beginning with support, editing, and astrological guidance. Clara Howard, a very special numerologist, gave me an outside reader's input, and an incredible numerology reading. And then there is Dick Schuettge, who taught me everything I needed to know about publishing. Thank you!

An endeavor such as this takes many people's energy, and I wish to acknowledge all who have taken part of their lifetimes to make this particular book happen in this magical time before the new millennium. Thank you for sharing your energies so generously.

1

Our Role as Women: Catalysts for Personal and Global Transformation

*The future belongs to those who believe
in the beauty of their dreams.*

ELEANOR ROOSEVELT

As we near the end of the twentieth century, we are called upon to embrace two primary aspects of life: living the personal dream we hold for ourselves while also making a contribution to the collective dream of a renewed and healthy planet.

The scope of this transformation may seem daunting and virtually impossible. How, you may ask, can I possibly bring about global change when I still struggle with the dynamics of my personal life—relationship, job, children, finances, parents, and so forth? Why is it necessary for me to take on the task of solving planetary problems when the leaders of the world can't seem to do it? Besides, others are dealing with global issues.

In this and subsequent chapters I will describe how our personal lives are intimately and irrevocably interconnected with the Earth and how the ecological crises, events in other parts of the world, and the imbalance of masculine and feminine energy at all levels affect our day-to-day lifestyles. And, conversely, how by embracing ourselves as women of power and substance in all arenas of our lives, we can be, *must be* — individually and collectively — a force for rectifying gender imbalance and healing the Earth.

It is important that you read this first chapter, as it creates the context and the container for all that follows. Before we can tackle our personal and relationship issues, we must see clearly how our everyday realities fit in the context of the big picture. We are now a global economy. The Internet and television bring the world into our living rooms; the work opportunities of our mates and ourselves are affected by the rise and fall of world currencies. The ecological crises and drastic changes in weather patterns directly affect the price of produce at the supermarket and the health and safety of our children and our families.

Many of the global issues that plague us are magnifications of personal issues. External ecology reflects internal ecology. Global issues *and* personal issues are both the consequence of the imbalance of male and female energies and the dominance of patriarchal agendas for centuries. They are also a function, in part, of our lack of understanding of how we as women are intimately connected with the Earth and her feminine energy.

Native American cosmology considers the Earth to be female and the Sun male. As the tribal Elders tell it, when the Sun and the Earth make love, the Earth gives birth and life is created. She births her plant children, then her animal children, and finally her human children. All her children are intimately interconnected and interrelated. From this teaching come two sacred laws: Everything is born of feminine energy. Nothing must be done to harm any of the Earth's children.

The tribal Elders prophesy that if humans honor these sacred laws, there will be harmony and balance on the Earth. On the other hand, if an imbalance manifests between the masculine and feminine energies, this will create disharmony and destruction. In our own lifetime, such an imbalance exists.

Almost universally known as Mother Earth or Grandmother Earth, our planet is a living, conscious female entity who gives birth to and sustains all life. Today, based on a scientific theory developed by James Lovelock, people often call her Gaia, the name of the ancient Greek Earth Goddess.

Grandmother Earth. Mother Earth. Gaia. Such is the essence and power of Earth's femaleness that until the seventeenth century the Earth was respected by European and other cultures as a living female being. It was from this understanding that thousands of cities, countries, and continents were given female names: Asia, Africa, Europe, Libya, Russia, Holland, China, Ireland, and more. In fact, the Earth's European names—Urth, Hertha, Eortha, Erda, and Hretha—all originate from the Sanskrit word Artha, which means "mater(mother)-ial wealth."[1]

However, due in part to the scientific and industrial revolutions of the last few centuries, we have become spiritually and psychologically disconnected from the Earth as a living planet. It wasn't until the 1970s and 1980s, when Lovelock developed the Gaia theory—the Earth as a self-regulating organism—that we collectively began to remember and reidentify with the Earth as our Mother.[2] The plants, animals, humans, the waters and the air, all are part of the living Earth, Gaia, all regulating and maintaining the necessary conditions to continue life on her. We are all part of the balance, all part of the whole. All of us are her children, for she births us all as part of her "give-away," to use an apt Native American expression.

Her plant children provide the key to life, the basis of the food chain. Plants draw energy from the sun and transform the energy into edible food for humans and animals. All who live closely connected with the Earth, including Native Americans and peoples from other indigenous cultures, recognize and respect this knowledge. The word *indigenous* actually means "belonging to the earth, by birth or by origin." The Elders say we are the Planet of the Children, where everything is born of female energy.

Women are thus indigenous to the Earth Mother. Like the Earth, we are capable of giving birth, of nurturing, of healing, of deep creativity. As women, we are walking embodiments of the great feminine power of the Earth. Spirit is born into women's blood; some simply call it intuition. As part of her, made in her energy image, we are able to function like her. We are pure perceivers of energy, which is our magical intuition. Our female energy births men into their higher energy centers, into their higher selves, and into their power.

We nurture others as the Earth nurtures us. We provide support as she supports us. We are her goddesses. This is the spiritual knowledge of oneness and connection. We carry the Earth's spiritual consciousness in our wombs. Women just *know*; that is the only way to explain it. And at some deep level we know we know! We women, the feminine energy, have been separated from the magical knowledge that Gaia gives each one of us power when we connect with her. Later in this book, I will guide you through an exercise to develop the awareness and power in your womb, which embodies this deep knowing. The strength of this knowing begins to stir within us and Mother Earth infuses us with feminine power which resides in our womb. Unfortunately, many men have been and are threatened when we remember this.

At this point in history, our worldwide political, economic, and religious institutions are still geared towards giving energy and planetary power to the energy of the masculine and towards repressing the feminine. Yet part of the success of masculine control has rested on ridding women's culture of the knowledge of their history, their connection, and their power. In the past, women's culture was carried on and taught by the older wise women. Yet this passing on of knowledge and wisdom from generation to generation was severely disrupted during the Inquisition, a 200-year period in history during the Middle Ages when up to nine million women, children, and homosexuals were burned as witches. Many of them were wise female elders or those who carried women's knowledge as leaders of their clan or their village.

The older wise woman also carries the knowledge of the strategies that the masculine energies use for control. She also knows their weaknesses. This is why, in today's world, the aging woman is robbed of her value, so that younger women will not listen to her or learn from her. Yet for women to come together to balance masculine energies, we have to remember our deep energetic connection to one another and to the Earth, and to gain strength from both.

As we evaluate history, we find a tremendous imbalance in masculine priorities in relation to Mother Earth and her give-away— her resources. However, indigenous peoples see the Earth's resources as part of her body. The soil is the skin of Mother Earth; the rocks are her bones; the gems, her organs; the rivers, her veins; and the crystals, her brain cells. Yet due to industrialization and overdevelopment, Mother Earth has been raped of her resources. Industry and business influences have become disproportionate to the power of ordinary people.

> *All of our fates are tied together. If the boat sinks,*
> *the whole boat sinks, not just half the boat.*

DR. ANTONIO NOVELLE, Former Surgeon General

The Elders say that when negative masculine rule dominates any part of Mother Earth, that part will become sterile. She will not give birth, and the land will turn barren; it will become a desert. This is happening today, in the process known as desertification. All over the planet the land is becoming barren because of disregard for the soil, overuse of chemicals, and increasing overpopulation. Experts estimate that 480 billion tons of topsoil have been lost.[3] Deserts have grown by fourteen million acres.[4]

Thus, the prophecies concerning imbalance are coming to pass in our own lifetime. With a rapidly deteriorating ozone layer due to pollution, the Earth is losing its protection against the sun's harmful ultraviolet rays.[5] Marine, animal, and plant life, which provide the basis for human survival, are threatened. Human beings also face the direct danger of increasing cancers and suppression of the human immune system.

Increasing evidence has become available to document the trend of global warming. According to meteorologists, the 1990s are becoming the warmest decade on record (the warmest years so far in the twentieth century took place in 1990, 1995, and 1997).[6] This warming trend is altering our weather patterns, our water supplies, and our crop yields.

According to an article in *Time* magazine, global warming is even reaching into the pockets of American insurance companies. "Natural disasters during the 1980s were 94 percent more frequent than in the 1970s. While it is possible that such a jump falls within normal climatic variation, insurance executives realize that it also conforms with patterns predicted for global warming."[7]

Another huge problem is deforestation. In fact, the Native American Elders' prophecies included the warning "The trees are falling" as one of the first signs of the Earth's destruction. Now trees are being cut down for profit both in rain forests and pine forests around the world, and acid rain contributes to the deforestation of millions of acres.

The grave danger to life on Earth became so evident that in the early 1990s some 1,600 scientists, including 102 Nobel Laureates, signed "A Warning to Humanity," which reads in part: "No more than one or a few decades remain before the chance to avert the threats we now confront will be lost and the prospects for humanity immeasurably diminished. . . . A new ethic is required—a new attitude towards discharging *our responsibility* for caring for ourselves and for the Earth. . . . This ethic must motivate a great movement, convincing reluctant leaders and reluctant governments and reluctant peoples themselves to effect the needed changes."[8]

As women, *we* are called upon to begin this great movement, just as we have initiated so many other movements.

In *Now It's Our Turn,* I suggest that it is our time, as women and as carriers of the female energy, to take our responsibility for balancing masculine energies and saving our home, planet Earth, for future generations. It is *our* generation, *now,* that will make the final decisions on the fate of life on Earth. We do not have another twenty or thirty years to waste. The rain forests are being cut down *now.* The ozone layer is being destroyed *now.* The oceans, lakes, and waters of the Earth are being polluted *now.* The air is being filled with chemicals and pollutants *now.* Our friends the animals are being driven into extinction *now.* And all this is taking place in the name of economic progress!

Another Native American teaching says that before deciding on any course of action, we must consider the effects of our actions on our children for seven generations to come. How will our grandchildren and our grandchildren's children describe the history of our time? How will our decisions today affect them? Will the history books of the future read like the following?

In the late twentieth century, the people of Earth, our ancestors, polluted themselves and the Earth for all future generations. They did this because of their greed and because they were afraid to suffer any material or economic changes in their standard of living. The United States and other industrialized countries were leaders in polluting the world, almost destroying life on Earth. This destruction of Nature was viewed as successful business progress. The accumulation of wealth became more important than the natural world, more important than the Earth itself. People became so greedy that they forgot they were destroying their own home.

Today, our intolerable heat, the high rate of cancer, and the fact that our children can no longer run and play outdoors are due to the near destruction of the ozone layer which once protected the Earth from the sun's ultraviolet rays. Global overheating and destruction of the ozone layer are due to twentieth-century people's extremely high use of fossil fuels and chlorofluorocarbons to maintain their lifestyles of overconsumption. Their factories poured out poisonous smoke and toxins, creating acid rain, along with air, water, and soil pollution.

Millions of species of animals, which we now consider a rarity, became extinct. The healing powers of many species of trees and flora were lost forever due to the destruction of the forests, particularly the rain forests, which once encircled the planet around the equator. We and our children now die of diseases that might have been cured with medicines from the rich array of plants that once grew there.

In addition, our Earth is covered with toxic waste sites from the production of nuclear weapons and power. These are the most contaminated of their legacies. They are lethal to us still and will be to our children's children for centuries to come.

Cruelty to their own offspring was so high that every year 15 million children died worldwide due to hunger and related diseases, even though there was plenty of food. Every year they killed 13 million domestic animals, and sent hundreds of thousands of their horses to be slaughtered. They denied the sacredness and interconnectedness of all life forms.

They did not recognize their greed and selfishness until it was too late for themselves, as well as for us. They destroyed our once beautiful home, planet Earth.

How do you feel when you read this? Do you experience a hint of shame or sadness? What we do today, as women, could change this story, but first we must break through our great denial and recognize how this crisis came to be.

The dynamic is basic. As women, we have been giving away our power; we have been allowing our energy and our strength to be submerged and repressed. Years of patriarchal domination have taken their toll. We have made relationships our main priority, neglecting much of what needs to be done on a larger scale. Many of us have wanted to be taken care of instead of taking responsibility for assuming our place of power alongside men. Paying attention to our personal lives, including how we function in our intimate relationships and in our families, and making changes to empower ourselves have become necessary not only to make our lives more satisfying but to ensure that we are firmly rooted in our power as we work to restore the balance of feminine and masculine energies in the world at large.

While the contemporary imbalance of masculine energy over feminine energy has been in place for centuries, it has not always been the reality. At one point in world history, women gathered together and were very powerful. We were leaders in all areas of society. Now is the moment for us to come forward again and bring the remembrance of those times to the forefront. Our power and strength are encoded in the recesses of our cells, waiting only to be reawakened. Now is the time to arise out of our long sleep.

We are at a pivotal point in our history. It is time for women to begin to claim the positive aspects of the feminine so that the positive aspects of the masculine can be born. Because it is important to face current reality if we are to bring true transformation, much of the information in the Awakening chapters of this book focuses on negative dimensions of masculine domination as it has manifested over the past centuries and in our own time. It is also important to acknowledge the positive potential of male energy when it comes forth, not to dominate but to guide with strength and courage. Just as each man has an inner feminine side, so each woman has an inner masculine aspect. This inner masculine side needs to be trained to support the feminine and exist in harmony with it.

To bring about this new partnership between masculine and feminine, we need to begin to reevaluate our personal relationships with men. We can only take our power in the world once we have reclaimed our power in our personal lives. This requires that we redefine our old domesticated roles within our home. Changes in the workplace are also crucial, so that, coming from our full strength and creativity we can influence corporate decisions for life and renewal, rather than for destruction, pollution, and the death of life.

Ultimately, our fate depends on connecting with women all over the world. We need to see ourselves in one another, and we need to help one another to escape from the repression of masculine-dominated cultures, religions, and governments. We women, representing feminine energy, must be free again to balance the energy of the Earth on a global scale.

You do not have to accomplish everything in this book to make a difference in your personal life and the life of the planet. If each one of us simply makes one real, true change, that alone will begin the process of changing the world as a whole.

PART ONE

Our Personal Lives

About Part One

M uch has been written about *men* — how to understand them, how to know their secrets, and how we, as women, should relate to them. In my years as a psychotherapist, I have witnessed over and over the struggle of women trying to learn how to be with and adjust to others, especially men. The emotional fallout has been frustration and loneliness.

Part One of this book is about how we as women participate in our relationships with men, while handling our numerous roles, and how this is interconnected with our economic and legal status, as well as the very survival of our planet.

If we perceive our problems as personal, and believe that we are the only ones with such problems, we are weakened. Believing our problems to be purely personal undermines our self-image and our self-confidence, and hypnotizes us into a false sense of helplessness. We come to believe that we can't control, overcome, or solve our problems, and depression sets in.

But if we share our problems and our secrets as women, realizing that many situations in our lives are determined by our culture and are shared by millions of other women like ourselves, this very process encourages us to solve the problems instead of attacking and blaming ourselves for being helpless. Our loneliness begins to dissolve. We begin to take positive action together.

In order to balance the masculine energies and shift the consciousness of the planet for the survival of Mother Earth, we need to begin to change our personal relationships. Because of our unfulfilled need for intimacy, women have been overly focused on our personal relationships with men. We've clung to Cinderella-like myths of how our relationships should be. Because we've been trained to focus so much of our attention on relationships, we have left crucial issues that are affecting the planet in the hands of men.

Before you read further, please note that Part One focuses on women in relationships with men. I'm well aware that some of the women who will read this book may be single or may be in primary relationships with other women. If you're single, you will probably still be able to relate to much of the material in this section. If you're lesbian, these heterosexual dynamics still define much of the world around you. Please take what is of value in deepening your understanding, and feel free to skip parts that are not as relevant. All of us have an important role to play in awakening feminine energy and bringing it into greater balance. Remember that the purpose of this examination is to allow us to free our energy and balance our personal lives so we can then step forward more fully into the public arena.

2

Awakening to the Reality
of Our Relationships

*Romantic-love relationships are made or broken by
the effectiveness or ineffectiveness of communication. The
essence of mutual self-disclosure is communication. And no
element of communication is more important to romantic
love than that of feelings and emotions.*

NATHANIAL BRANDEN, PH.D.,
The Psychology of Romantic Love

Most women spend at least 75 percent of their waking lives focused on relationship. Has this investment of time and energy been worth it? Have we spent so much time worrying about being in relationship that we have disregarded the larger perspective of our lives and the problems and needs of the world around us? Let us take a look at how we have fared in our relationships with men.

We Are Lonely Women

*I really feel lonely in my relationship. I try to fulfill myself
with me, the kids, my career, and my friends, but I am still lonely
inside. I try to do all the things they say to do: be a feminine*

woman, be a nurturing mother, be supportive of my husband,
create a warm home, and have a job. But I still get lonely and
tired.

It's hard to let go of the romantic fantasies I had before we
were married. I dreamt of a man I could share everything with.
We would be lovers and intimate friends. We would talk for hours
and share our deepest feelings. He was more like that in the be-
ginning; then it became different.

He feels uncomfortable with my emotions and now with my
attempts to share my feelings. Talking about our relationship seems
to disturb him. He just seems to distance himself in so many ways.
He seems uncomfortable with deep or intimate feelings.

Natalie

Many of us have experienced such loneliness, such disconnection from our partner. Because of our socialization and perhaps even our inherent energy patterns, relationships are often
the primary focus of our being as women. Yet for many of us,
our fantasy lover never retained his substance after the first two
years. As one woman shared, "It's different than I thought it
would be—I had visions of warmth and intimacy, not distance
and separation."

Why are women lonely in so many of our relationships with
men? Women are very different from men. We express ourselves
more emotionally and verbally in relationships; we make ourselves more vulnerable. Women tend to be communicators, and
we communicate about feelings. In general, we enjoy sharing,
talking, opening up, and being close.

According to clinical psychologist Georgia Witkin, Ph.D.,
"Most women are raised to please other people and to take care of
them." She says that women "seem to have a higher sensitivity than
men to verbal cues, and consequently we're more likely to hear
other people's needs and listen for their approval than men are."[1]

When we try to make a deeper emotional connection with the men in our lives, we are often told that we are being too emotional or "too heavy." Because some men judge any show of emotions to be a sign of weakness, they prefer to live on the surface, in denial of their feelings. They shut us out, and the harder we knock on the door, the more tightly they hold it closed.

"When I start expressing feelings or wanting to talk about our relationship, he gets irritable. I can see him getting nervous. He shuts me off quickly with a short comment, or he leaves the room," said one former client, Shannon.

The problem is almost universal. In her study *Women and Love,* Shere Hite found that 98 percent of her female subjects wanted "more verbal closeness with the men they love; they want the men in their lives to talk more about their own personal thoughts, feelings, plans and questions, and to ask them about theirs; 83 percent of the women say they initiate most deep talks—and try very hard to draw men out; 71 percent of the women say the men in their lives are afraid of emotion; and 63 percent of women meet with great resistance when they try to push their husband or lover to talk about feelings."[2]

Most men are threatened by intimacy, while most women are threatened by separation. The resulting pain of this disconnection is loneliness, frustration, and the feeling that there is something wrong with us as women for being more emotional and more focused on relationship.

Marriage in general is experienced by women much differently than it is experienced by men. According to author Jessie Bernard in the book *The Future of Marriage,* "Because we are so accustomed to the way in which marriage is structured in our society, it is hard for us to see how different the wife's marriage really is from the husband's, and how much worse." She continues: "There is considerable research literature reaching back over a generation which shows that: More wives than husbands consider their marriages unhappy, have considered separation or divorce, have regretted their marriages; and fewer report positive companionship." To conclude, she notes: "It is not the complaints of wives that demonstrate how bad the wife's marriage is, but rather the poor mental and emotional health of married women as compared not only to the health of married men's but also to unmarried women's."[3] Bernard's book was written in 1972 and revised in 1982, but the same problem exists today. In the late 1990s, this research was again validated, as noted in the *Menninger Letter*, which reported that marital distress is more evident in wives. Married men are less affected by recent gender and family role changes than women, which put extra strains on the relationship due to women's dual roles.[4]

Emotional Support

A relationship represents a commitment we make to another person in which we try to fulfill the other person's needs as well as our own within the energies of our union. Yet, many women find an imbalance in the support or nurturing they give in comparison to what they receive. Most women have shared with me that they feel they do most of the nurturing work in their relationships with men.

Feminine energy attracts men, since they usually find it very healing as we nurture and support them. Women try to help men "become" their ideals. We take on their dreams and make them our own. We encourage our men, as well as become their financial partners. Sometimes we even support them in the early part of their careers. We take care of their physical needs and comforts. Do we receive the support, encouragement, and nurturing that we give to our partners?

Because men are so uncomfortable with their feelings, women have often been men's "emotional caretakers." We put a tremendous amount of energy into nurturing men's egos and giving them emotional support. According to Dr. Shaevitz, former director of the Institute for Family and Work Relationships, "Women supply to their husbands twice as much emotional support as they receive." This is because women have been socialized and trained since childhood to be "other-directed," while men have been trained to be more ego-directed. In essence, women take care of others' needs, while men are better at getting their own needs fulfilled.

Contrary to popular gender myths, men seem to need and depend on women for nurturing and support more than women depend on men. If it's true that husbands are less conscious in relationships and nurture less while wives nurture more, how does that leave us feeling?

In today's lifestyle of dual-career relationships, where both the wife and husband must work to support a family, women too require greater nurturing and emotional support. Otherwise we find that we give, give, give, and eventually we begin to resent it.

We feel lonely. We entered a relationship to care for and to be taken care of, and we end up taking care of everyone other than ourselves.

If our need for intimate relationship were fulfilled, women might feel a wholeness and an inner strength that would enable us to venture forth more fully into the world. After being satisfied emotionally within the relationship—just as men are being cared for, nurtured, and supported at home—we would be able to accomplish more in the world. Our perspective would broaden as we began to rely on the fulfillment of our relationships to provide the stable base to project ourselves out into the larger arena.

3

Solutions to Intimacy and Emotional Power

I gain strength, courage, and confidence by every experience in which I must stop and look fear in the face. . . . I say to myself, I've lived through this and can take the next thing that comes along. . . . We must do the things we think we cannot do.

ELEANOR ROOSEVELT

Our Relationships: Balancing Feminine and Masculine

Any therapist will tell you that women comprise the majority of clients seeking therapeutic help for their relationships. Books on how to improve every aspect of our relationships—from sexuality to intimacy—sell by the millions, especially to women. We keep trying to fix, fuel, heal, motivate, repair, understand, and change our relationships to meet our myths, fantasies, and needs. We all are basically beating our heads against a brick wall; we cannot mold our relationships into what we have been told to expect—living intimately "happily ever after." This chapter will further deepen your understanding of this dynamic, and present solutions for true intimacy and emotional power.

The Death of the Princess Myth

The myth of the damsel being rescued by Prince Charming and living happily ever after is dead! A whole world of women watched as our most cherished myth ended tragically for a number of highly visible women over the last two decades. We all watched as several "princesses" went through very difficult times in their individual fairy tales. Prince Charming didn't save them.

After the fairy tale weddings were over, these women were lonely. The romance gone and the myth shattered, these women had to turn inward to find the strength inside themselves to save themselves. No one was going to take care of them, especially emotionally.

I believe that at least one of these women, Princess Diana, grew to understand this reality before her untimely death. Her life sends a message to us all that the tremendous energy we put into relationship must be redirected and put out into the world. Princess Diana found the strength in herself to make a difference in the world, to stand up and care for the poor and to embrace important causes such as the movement to end AIDS and to prevent land mines from claiming further innocent lives.

Princess Diana set an example for us to grow into our own power and to use that power for the good of all. She faced her fears and went beyond her relationship, her home, and her country to help others and stand up for what she believed in. She took risks in the face of criticism and disapproval. She chose to take her own power and make a difference in the world.

We, too, can learn to shift our primary focus from our relationship with men to our relationship with our own inner power, which can then be manifested outward to change the world and possibly even save the planet.

Balancing Our Attitude
and Approach to Relationships

We are brought up with many Cinderella-like myths concerning men, relationship, marriage, and children, with the predominant myth being that having a relationship and/or being married is the answer to all our problems. Then, after we marry, we cannot figure out why we are not living "happily ever after" with our mate.

Women's lives have been imbalanced. We have based too much of our lives on our need for fulfillment in relationships. This is not the result of biological predestination, but of our social conditioning. We need to find a realistic set of values and beliefs concerning men, marriage, and relationships, and let go of our princess myths.

How can we achieve this? First, we need to realize that our lives can be full and abundant with our own energy. Men can add to that energy, but they shouldn't become the desperate focus of our lives. We need to find happiness within our own being, with our own achievements, with connecting to one another, and through involvement in the global arena. The smaller our lives become, the more lonely, dependent, and unhappy we tend to be.

Second, we must recognize that we cannot force a man to be intimate with us; we will most likely overwhelm him with fear, and he will pull away. To create the intimacy we desire, we need to find inner solutions for ourselves and within ourselves, and then manifest these solutions in our relationships and in the world. We must become like magnets that attract energy. This requires work on our own energy. To move towards these solutions, we must examine our old attitudes and beliefs about love, romance, relationships, and marriage.

Romance

Research has shown that the stage of highest romance in a relationship is usually the first eighteen to twenty-four months. Thereafter, life and love change in the relationship. It is useful to take a look at the word *romantic.* The definition is "Excitingly or enticingly different or unusual." And some synonyms are "Exotic, strange."[1] So how can we expect to wake up day after day, year after year, with the same person and have an enticingly different, strange, and exotic relationship? It is difficult if not impossible! Yet we compare our whole married life to that first period of heightened romance.

If we get stuck in the "time warp" of expecting our relationship to be like the first eighteen months, we will always be unhappy. This reflects an immature view of reality. The truth is, all relationships change. We can mature and accept the change as growth, or we can go through several marriages, always looking for that "romantic high," ending relationships by saying, "I love him, but I'm not in love with him." Growing up and maturing means realizing our own potential and not living off the high drama of "the relationship," but balancing relationship to be a wonderful, loving part of our lives, not something that consumes 90 percent of our waking moments. We need to create our own world of being, our own sense of self in a larger context.

Love and romance are really two separate issues. Harry Stack Sullivan, a famous psychiatrist, defines love thus: "When the satisfaction or the security of another person becomes as significant to one as one's own satisfaction or security, then the state of love exists."[2] This definition describes individuals who are functioning in relation to each other as equals. In marriages that have lasted many years, the key ingredient is not passionate, romantic love, but "tolerance, respect, honesty and the desire to stay together for mutual advantage." These are the four elements researchers have found in long-term successful marriages, relationships that mature with time.[3]

Living in Illusion About Men

So often, women are living in an illusion with regard to our expectations about men. Our real partners are very different from our fantasies. We have many expectations of men that they cannot meet due to their socialization.

In our imbalanced, dysfunctional culture, men have been brought up to shut down the caring, emotional side of themselves. They are considered weak, "feminine," and indecisive if they come across as too emotional or intimate. Many men have learned to function from their heads, from a logical, ordered perspective of the world. They lack the fluidity of emotion and communication skills that women have learned. Men have been allowed to express themselves through sexuality and anger because these are considered aggressive, "masculine" traits. But they have not been allowed to actively express their emotions, such as grief, sadness, or intimacy.

Some men have become robots to the economy, their corporations, and "their team," and in the process many have lost their souls. No wonder they have to shut down day after day to survive. If they truly let another in, it might hurt too much to be alive in the concrete, logical life they have been trying to lead.

According to matriarchal cultures, such as many Native American cultures, the Elders teach that female energy awakens men to their higher spiritual self and inner connections. "All Gods are born from the womb of a Goddess." But in our industrialized society, women no longer have men's respect to guide men in this way. Therefore, men do not take us seriously when we try to awaken them to intimacy or spirituality.

Finding Solutions: Allowing

Women must take back our own power so we can set men free as well. This means rising to our full potential and letting go of our desperation. We must change ourselves, our attitudes, and our approach so that the new dynamics will offer the opportunity of change to others around us. We need to allow men to be who they are, without bashing them into meeting our expectations for intimacy and communication. Currently, within the more enlightened aspects of the Men's Movement, many men are taking a look at themselves and trying to change either on their own or with the support of other men. We must recognize that men have to find their "inner being" on their own. The harder we push, the more they will resist, so *allowing* becomes an especially important principle.

Allow your male partner to be who he is; leave him alone. Stop battering him for intimacy, for that's precisely what many of us have been doing. Give him credit and appreciation for his strengths. Just allow him to "be," as you work on balancing and increasing your own female power. Concentrate on your own growth.

Men generally see life as a set of challenges, and after they have won their princess, their focus of attention shifts to going out into the world to provide for her. This is what they have learned growing up, and most take their responsibility seriously. Their focus of attention changes to the challenge outside their relationships, which leaves us feeling abandoned and full of self-pity. But given the current reality, this is the natural course of events in a man's life.

As women, we need to acquire emotional balance by learning how to fulfill our own needs. If you need something in a desperate way, it will run from you. As we gain deep inner happiness and peace within ourselves, we can then bring that strength and balance to our relationships. We then become more magnetic, instead of desperate, drawing in male energy rather than overwhelming our partner by asking so insistently for it. Remember, being in your center *is* power, and feminine power will actually pull men closer.

This shift of focus—from expecting men to fulfill our inner needs to taking responsibility for our inner fulfillment—allows more intimacy and balances the power in our relationships.

Creating Emotional Balance

Women need to learn to balance our emotions with maturity and a keen sense of reality. The first rule of staying balanced is to observe the reality of a situation and to remain in the role of observer, which means above the drama, so we can see the dynamics clearly and act from our center. This state requires maturity, and it creates magic. We women *are* magic when we stay centered and take our power. We can create change. We lose power when we become histrionic, which means "of or relating to drama," or overdramatic with our emotions.[4] Can you feel the difference intuitively?

EAGLE OR MOUSE?

In this visualization, imagine in your mind's eye an eagle soaring high above the Earth below. From the eagle's vantage point, the entire landscape is visible, and her sharp eyes see with great clarity.

Now imagine a tiny mouse nestled up against the root of a large tree. She is aware of the immediate details around her, but she can't see what's on the other side of the tree or even over a large root extending out from the trunk.

Learn to see with clarity, and be like the eagle who flies high above the world and observes the situation below in its entirety. From her lofty position, the eagle observes the dynamics and interconnection of all energy, while the little mouse, in contrast, sees only what is in front of her, and the slightest change can throw her into a crisis, because to the mouse everything looks so big!

Are you a mouse or an eagle?

As you reflect on your experience of the eagle and the mouse, remember that the goal is to learn *not to react* to another's behavior. For example, men often use language to give themselves the upper hand while women take verbal assaults personally.[5] To throw women off balance and gain control of a situation, men unconsciously know that all they have to do is to act in a way or say something in a manner to trigger us to become emotional. Once men have gotten us into an emotional state, they know we will become unbalanced and lose touch with reality. This state pulls us out of clarity. Men then go straight to their head and exercise logic to try to prove us wrong. Then they have the power and control in the situation.

Women then escalate our emotions as we attempt to get our mate to understand and hear us. The situation becomes one of unbalanced reaction. We feel as if we are going nuts! The minute you are at the effect of a man's words or actions, you have given your power away and allowed him to grab your energy. Does this sound familiar? You can change this pattern by remembering the larger vision of the eagle and recognizing the tactics used to throw your energy off balance. Reconnecting with your center is another crucial component in changing these dynamics.

Awakening Womb Power and Holding the One-Point: How to Develop Emotional Balance, Mental Clarity, and Physical Presence

Many of the world's great traditions, including the Native American, the yogic, and the Buddhist traditions, have taught a variation of a fundamental centering technique. Martial arts students learn this technique to center themselves and hold their balance and power.

I learned this practice from the American Indian teachings. The grandmothers teach this technique to women to help them learn to hold their space and stay centered around and with male energy. As one writer working in the Asian tradition describes this centered state: "A shallow river is constantly turbulent, but it is difficult to make waves on a deep one."[6]

AWAKENING WOMB POWER

This exercise may be used as a meditation by itself or as an ongoing exercise to help you stay emotionally balanced and mentally clear throughout the day and in any situation.

It is vitally important in the midst of our busy schedules to find some alone time every day, even if that is only a five-minute meditation. Whether you do it just before going to bed at night, upon rising in the morning, or snatching a few precious minutes during the day, the length of time is not so important as the relaxation and focus you develop through ongoing practice.

If you use it as a meditation exercise, create a sacred place, a place that is quiet, protected, and comfortable; a place where you won't be interrupted. This may be a room in your home, in your garden, a quiet area in a local park, wherever. As you develop your ability to concentrate, you will be surprised to find that you can do this in a crowded mall!

1. Begin by sitting comfortably in a relaxed but upright position. Close your eyes and focus your attention on your breathing; just notice the rhythm of your breath. Clear your mind of mental chatter by allowing any thoughts to move through your mind. Don't stop and focus on a particular thought or inner voice. If you find yourself doing this, just let it go and continue to relax.

2. Then begin to breathe more deeply. As you inhale, visualize drawing light, energy, grace, spirit, and love into your body. Hold each inhalation for just a moment; feel the energy permeate your whole body. Then exhale, and as you do so visualize that outflow of breath cleansing your body by taking with it all the toxins, the stress and tensions, the upsets, and any negative energy that you are holding. Relax into the exhalation. Repeat this several times or until you feel relaxed.

3. Now move your awareness to the area of your womb. Put your hand on this area and drop your energy and focus there. You may experience your awareness having a weight of its own which falls gently down through the center of your body until it rests in your womb area.

4. Inhale into and exhale from your womb. As you inhale just as before, visualize your womb expanding with light, energy, grace, spirit, love, power, and wisdom. Visualize this expansion until you are one large pulsating womb of power. You are pregnant with infinite possibility, creativity, and beauty. You are the human personification of the Earth Mother. *Now think from your womb and feel from your womb.* Do you feel a difference? Don't make this process difficult; its essence is very simple. Continue this for

a minute or so or until you can feel that difference. Embrace this experience until you feel centered.

This practice centers you, grounds you, and enables you to utilize this most important aspect of yourself. Our womb is the birthing place not just for physical children, but of our creativity, our intuitive knowing. It is our connection to the Earth Mother.

HOLDING THE ONE-POINT

You may practice this technique any time, anywhere, but of course, it is best to practice where you will not be interrupted. You will develop your ability faster if you work with a partner or at least ask a friend to test your progress periodically.

1. Concentrate your focus of attention again in your womb area, but this time on a spot about two inches below your navel. This is called your one-point, or your center of gravity. Native traditions also call it your "shamanic root of power." Place your hand on this spot and poke it gently or apply pressure there.

2. Breathe into this spot. Inhale. Exhale. Focus every part of your being into that point, as though all of you — your heart, mind, body, and spirit — is condensed there. Then, "think on the underside," that is, visualize all of you concentrated in your one-point firmly rooted or anchored in the earth. You might think of a heavy bowling ball hanging down from your one-point that pulls your weight down and anchors you. The technique of focusing on the one-point is used in martial arts to prevent your opponent from throwing you off balance and moving you out of position. Holding your one-point, you are immovable.

3. Test your progress in this focus by having someone try to physically push your body off balance. As you get better

at this, you will be amazed at how centered you become. It will also enable you to conserve energy during the day.

4. Be aware of holding your energy in your womb and your one-point throughout the day to help you stay calm and centered. If you forget, just gently drop your awareness there again. A calm mind creates a calm body and vice versa.

Now translate the effects of these two exercises into the emotional and mental challenges that confront you. As you continue to practice, you will develop the ability to do this instantaneously. When an emotionally charged situation erupts or you are tensing in a stressful moment and you feel yourself being pushed off your center, quickly drop your focus into your womb and your one-point, breathe deeply, and ground yourself. You will find an immediate shift in your energy, your mind will clear, and you can then respond to the situation from the feminine wisdom and intuitive knowing of your womb, and the steady anchor of your one-point.

When we come from our heart all the time, we burn out emotionally. When we come from our head all the time, intellectualizing and analyzing, we become mentally exhausted. Women's true power and energy comes from our womb area. When our energy comes from this area, we have magical stamina and inner strength. We "know" who we are, and we remain in full command of our power, our inner authority.

The power I am describing is not about controlling or seeking to control others. Power can be defined in terms of your ability to act. Each subsequent act builds on that power. Power is the ability of a living being to perform in a given way for a particular purpose. This is what we women need in our lives and in our world: We need power and the ability to act in order to balance feminine and masculine energies and improve our lives while helping to save planet Earth.

Overcoming Dependence and Self-Pity

Women surrender our individuality and autonomy more in love relationships than in any other sphere. Every moment you surrender your free will, you lose energy. As a psychotherapist, I am still surprised at the number of professional women I see in my practice who want to be taken care of financially. This is many women's secret dream. Each of us has been born into this time of transition for a reason. Many of us are being pushed into creating financial independence for ourselves, whether we are married or single, because this is the true test of power. Women of this generation have to learn independence so we can meet the collective challenges that face our planet. We need the financial freedom to create our visions and dreams without the limitations of the negative pole of male energy. We are here to establish the strengths of feminine energies at this pivotal point in history.

Quite often, wanting to be taken care of, the little girl part of us falls into a victim-martyr syndrome. Once this happens, we lose our energy and power. We project our problems and pour our anger onto others instead of taking responsibility for our own lives. "He's not fulfilling my needs" becomes our mantra.

Let go of your emotional dependencies on another to fulfill your life, your needs, and your soul. When you define your own identity through others outside of yourself, you lose sight of your own being and mastery. When you lose your own spirit, others don't see it either. You can easily drop into self-pity. Self-pity is a powerful force that spirals us swiftly down and pulls us out of our center. This is one of the worst traps, and it is easy for us as women to fall into it with men and relationships. But we lose our feminine power and ability when we do. Self-pity only absorbs our own energy.

FEEDING YOUR SPIRIT

Our world is a reflection, like a mirror, of our beliefs, attitudes, and concepts. Our perception of ourselves and our personal world can be changed from within. Become conscious of the thoughts you are feeding yourself, for your thoughts are your spirit's food. You can gauge the kind of thoughts you are thinking by how you feel. For example, if you feel depressed, you are feeding your spirit negative, self-pitying, or sad thoughts.

The thoughts you feed yourself will determine how you feel, as well as influence your self-esteem, your health, and your self-confidence. How you feel determines the vibrations that you emanate into the world, your magnetism. These vibrations, in turn, determine what you will attract back to yourself. This is a circular process.

You can achieve the experience of true power by becoming aware of the thoughts you are feeding your spirit. Practice observing your thoughts for an hour, then for a day. It is all right if you forget: Just wake yourself up and start over again. You might want to record what you've learned in a journal at the end of the day.

Whatever you do, don't beat yourself up with your thoughts. The world is tough enough without us beating on ourselves! Be gentle and forgiving with yourself. You'd give the same kindness to a child, a friend, or an animal. Praise yourself every time you wake yourself up!

What we experience in life is basically our own inner feelings.

SWAMI CHIDVILA SANANDA

To create the intimacy we desire, we first have to turn inward and look at ourselves. We need to take our strengths and be ourselves fully. Such self-actualization creates a magnet and helps us to balance ourselves and the feminine principle in our relationships and in the world. Capturing the power of the feminine energy in our relationships will balance the masculine and shift our relationships into a healthier place.

To recapture the important points of this chapter:

1. Change your attitude and approach to relationships. Examine your old belief systems, and look closely at the reality of your relationships with men.

2. How addicted have you been to relationships with men? What percentage of your life have they taken up?

3. Have you *allowed* men to be who they are? Have you learned acceptance?

4. Create emotional balance for yourself by learning to stay centered and remain in the observer role when men try to trigger you into your emotions. Stay in *clarity about reality,* like the eagle. Don't be a mouse!

5. By dropping your energy to your womb area and learning to hold your one-point, you reclaim your female power and can remain calm and centered in emotional situations.

6. Allow men to "be" and to have space until they are more comfortable with intimacy and themselves.

7. Rise out of the trap of self-pity and the victim/martyr syndrome. Become aware of the thoughts you are feeding your spirit. Nourish yourself with self-affirming thoughts.

8. Push your edge to become who you are: creative, intelligent, powerful. This will magnetize people to you. You will be able to accomplish anything.

9. Remember, power attracts; neediness distances.

4

Awakening to Our Sexuality

Women give sex for love. Men give love for sex.

Dr. Tony Grant

Women and Sexuality

Lovemaking can be like touching souls. For women, passionate sexuality begins with the emotional, sensual, and communicative content of the relationship. It can be a romantic interlude that begins hours before actual intercourse with emotional intimacy, touching, and closeness. This is not to say we need emotional attachment to physically have an orgasm. The average female can come to orgasm within four minutes if the circumstances are supportive.

Yet, many of us are quietly and secretly unhappy in our sexual relationships. When women have unmet emotional needs in their relationships, it is difficult for us to connect sexually in a meaningful way. When we finally get discouraged trying to connect, we often leave relationships sexually. We then lose the sense of bonding and attachment. We no longer want to be so intimately vulnerable to someone we cannot reach in a deeply emotional or spiritual way.

But many women feel responsible for sexually satisfying our partner, whether we want to have intercourse or not. As one woman told me, "I sometimes feel I just do my wifely duty with my husband." In the back of a woman's mind, there is almost always the nonverbalized fear or threat that if a husband is not satisfied at home, he will find sex elsewhere. In truth, 70 percent of married men have had outside affairs, and this is usually connected in some ways to sex. A common time for a husband's first affair is during the third trimester of a wife's pregnancy.

Men are sometimes unaware of a woman's physical needs. According to the still-classic *Hite Report on Female Sexuality,* the majority of women, about 70 percent, do not experience orgasm regularly from intercourse alone.[1] This may result from the different needs and expectations of the woman and the man. For example, foreplay can offer the major part of enjoyment and romantic connection for a woman, while some men have described it as a chore. Sexual preliminaries are often too brief, or men may not be knowledgeable enough concerning the individual woman's body and how to arouse her.

Due to the lack of intimate communication, couples often have a difficult time stating their physical needs and desires. Sometimes we hesitate to tell our lovers what we want for fear of hurting their male egos. Many women fake orgasms for this same reason. Inhibited sexual desire is now one of the most common sexual disorders. In some cases, the lack of desire can be traced to women giving up, closing down, and not wanting to be vulnerable to someone they can't share with on other levels. We lose our desire to be sexually close when we don't feel a balance of sharing. When our partner keeps us so separated emotionally, this kills the part of us that wants to become one through sexual expression. This kills our trust. Disillusionment leads to detachment.

In addition, fatigue, stress, and religious and cultural beliefs may interfere with a woman's sexuality. We play numerous roles as we try to fulfill the different obligations to everyone around us—to our job, our children, our parents, our friends, and our spouse. Most of today's women are exhausted and unbalanced in our physical and sexual selves. Awakening to our sexuality calls on us to reown all parts of ourselves as we begin to understand the tremendous force that is our sexual power.

Women's Unmet Emotional Needs = Men's Unmet Sexual Needs

In our sexual relationships, women stop trying to magnetize men physically when men disconnect from us emotionally. The "secret" that men overlook time and time again is that a woman's sexual drive is very psychological. Human sexuality researchers and popularizers Masters and Johnson pointed out more than thirty years ago that a woman's sexual willingness "requires a psychological go-ahead, a green light in the mind."[2]

Two separate research studies, one at Brown University Medical School and the other at Mount Sinai School of Medicine, concluded that women may show physiological signs of vaginal arousal if watching a sex film, but we do not always *feel* aroused at the same time. There is a difference between physical and psychological arousal in a woman's body and brain. Women tend to respond sexually to feeling, "not to instant cues, but atmosphere, all those collective cues that are signaling warmth, intimacy and absence of danger—attentiveness, a soothing voice, whispering, touching."[3]

When a woman's lover breaks the psychological and emotional bond, he also breaks the sexual bond. These go hand-in-hand for many women. And once that emotional bond is broken, from that day forward many women put sex in a different category; it becomes a chore, servicing, duty, and so on. Thus, it is crucial that we explain to our partners that they are sabotaging the very thing *they* want—sexual intimacy—by short-circuiting emotional or verbal communication. We can teach men the art of sensuousness, the art of creating intimacy. It is helpful to explain to our partner that sensual intimacy starts in the morning and flows through each hour together; it is not something that begins immediately before bedtime. If men can learn sensual intimacy, maybe we can learn to be more spontaneous sexually and to balance our sexual energies with each other. Communicating honestly is the first step, as we discuss more fully in the following chapter on solutions.

5

Solutions Through Understanding Our Sexual Power

A woman is a vehicle of life. Life has overtaken her. Woman is what it is all about—the giving of birth and the giving of nourishment. She is identical with the Earth goddess in her powers, and she has to realize that about herself.

JOSEPH CAMPBELL, *The Power of Myth*

In the last chapter, we looked at some of the ways emotional distance contributes to our sexual problems. Women's sexual freedom exists in direct relation to our individual and societal freedoms. Historically, when women have been repressed, a major focus of that repression has been control of our sexuality. It is important that we understand that sexuality is not confined to the genital area. Our sexuality involves our whole being, our energy of charisma and expansion, and most important, our power. There are many problems surrounding the exchange of sexual energy between women and men. This chapter continues to examine some of the major difficulties we encounter, along with proposing some solutions to these difficulties.

External Solutions: Communicating About Sex

Women have kept a secret for many generations: We haven't learned to communicate about our female sexuality with men. Some of us haven't been honest in our sexual relationships; we haven't let our lover know what we need or what brings us pleasure. Most of us fake orgasm from time to time. I recently asked a sexually healthy, orgasmic, and active seventy-eight-year-old female friend how many times in her life she had faked orgasm with her partners through the years. "So many times I couldn't count. I didn't want to hurt their feelings." We all know that secret! However, there are several other reasons we are not communicative or honest.

The major reason we are not honest about sexuality is because we are taking care of the male. We don't want to hurt his ego or his feelings. Sadly, we sacrifice our sexual selves to keep a man's sexual image intact. Unfortunately, this sacrifice does not lead to a better relationship. In fact, in the long term it leads to resentment and avoidance—resentment if we say yes and guilt if we say no.

It is imperative that we women learn to talk about sex with honesty. Men need to learn to verbalize emotionally, and women need to verbalize sexually instead of shutting down. We can take our sexual power back and make sure it is returned to us.

With regard to our body and the female sexual response, Masters and Johnson's sexual research revealed some interesting facts. After questioning 350 women on orgasm, they found most of the women rated orgasmic levels higher and more intense with self-masturbation than they did with sexual intercourse with their male partners. In fact, orgasm through intercourse was rated the least in intensity. This is partly due to the fact that we have fewer nerve endings around our vaginal opening, so that intercourse alone is not as stimulating.[1] But it is also due to the fact that we don't communicate to our lovers the sexual secrets about our bodies that we know and use ourselves. Each woman is unique and will have to teach her lover her secrets.

In addition to committing yourself to communicating honestly about sex, spend some time learning about your body. You are a beautiful expression of the feminine energy of nature. Women's sexual appetite can be increased with body acceptance and the stimulation of our imagination. Releasing sexual tension keeps you in good health, both mentally and physically. Learn to accept and love your own body.

As you learn about your body, also learn about your sexual responses. For example, did you know that there are four physiological states that your body experiences while making love? They are excitement, plateau, orgasm, and resolution. However, after orgasm, women return to the plateau stage before going to the resolution stage, while men go directly to the resolution stage. One of the reasons women love to be cuddled and loved after sex is because we are potentially multiorgasmic, and our bodies return to the plateau stage ready to make love again. We can go on to repeat orgasm.[2] This can be intimidating to men and is one reason that they try to control our sexuality through the culture.

Bonding

With the sexual freedoms of the current era, it is perhaps especially important that we be very careful who we make love to. *Current research indicates that sexual intercourse and orgasm may increase our need to bond with a particular male.* This can result in our bonding to very inappropriate men without carefully evaluating our relationship to who they are as people.

The sexual revolution both freed women from sexual captivity and confronted us with new challenges. Sexuality became our choice as free spirits, not just as married women. We owe it to ourselves to make these choices with full consciousness, realizing that when making physical love our emotional and spiritual aspects blend as well.

Inner Solutions:
Balancing Women's Unconscious Guilt and Shame

Control of female sexuality equals control of female freedom. Research shows that "religious belief is a particularly important part of our sexual experience. Researchers find that religion, more than any other sociological factor, plays the strongest influence on women's sexual behavior."[3]

For thousands of years, women have carried the shame and guilt for the fall of humanity into the duality of good and evil. Throughout the Western world, the biblical creation story has condemned women's sexuality. In the creation story of the Garden of Eden, Eve ate the forbidden fruit and assumed the blame for sexual consciousness. From that point on, a woman was portrayed as a sexual temptress who had to be controlled; otherwise, she would seduce men into evil. If we can be controlled through our sexuality, we will lose our power and our ability to act in the world.

The story of Adam and Eve emerged at a period in history that some archeologists believe to have been a time of political and spiritual change from a matrilineal culture with a female family lineage into a patriarchal or male-dominated culture. The serpent in the creation story, who counsels Eve to eat the apple, was actually the symbol of the goddess culture. With this shift, women had to be sexually controlled in order to ensure men's paternity so that the power, wealth, and control could be transferred from one man to the next, from father to son. For this reason, male babies came to be valued much more highly. With their birth, they carry male wealth, property, and power. The marriage bond ensured a man's right to "own a womb," and in addition made certain that "his woman" would not have sex with another man. This principle has been important to the continuation of male patriarchal culture.[4]

We need to question any religious doctrine that allows men to make the rules to limit women's sexual or spiritual powers. In this way, we can overcome false guilt and enjoy our sexual and spiritual lives more fully.

Owning Your Sexual Pride:
Breaking Free From Shame

Whatever our religious beliefs, women need to realize that shame and sin should not be connected or attached to the beautiful process of creating life or to our body, which creates it. If we look around us, all of Mother Nature is a powerful feminine sexuality who pulls to her and recreates in her beauty all the children of the Earth—the plants, animals, and human beings. Women are a part of this powerful energy, and we are aligned with the great creator, the Earth Mother.

The American Indians say, "Everything is born of feminine energy."[5] If we break free with our spirits, we can learn to tap into that free, powerful, creative energy that births not only children but ourselves into the realm of the mysterious female energy that makes all of creation continuous from century to century. This includes all women, whether we birth physical children as an earth mother, or birth our own creativity, originality, or free will, or birth these characteristics in others, as a universal mother.

We are called upon to recognize and realize that we are healthy, powerful, multiorgasmic sexual beings, reflecting the very essence of Mother Earth. It is this energy that men have so often tried to tame and conquer.

Institutions that grasp for power have created guilt around healthy, normal sexuality, because when people feel guilty about themselves, they can more easily be controlled. They then have to go outside of themselves to a person of power to be cleansed of their "sins," giving away their own power in the process. When we seek outside of ourselves and our own connection to our own god, we will always remain uncentered, in fear, and reactive, easily controlled and manipulated.

It is time to take back our sexual power, and not be guilty, ashamed, or afraid of it. We must not give it away to please or get another's approval, and we must not let our sexuality be manipulated and used to control us. Sexuality and creation are our unending gift to future generations of humanity. Therefore, we must honor ourselves.

Did you know that the true meaning of the word *virgin* comes from the Latin root meaning "strength, force, and skill"? True virginity is the ability to take care of yourself within your own space. Awaken the energy of the true virgin within you. Awaken your body, your mind, and your spirit to the creative energy of your own sexual power. Let your strength roar within you. Don't be afraid of or ashamed of yourself. You can take care of yourself. It is always the woman who chooses, who can say yes or no, when she has this power.

Awaken the fire of the true virgin. Female energy is the power that recreates all of humanity. The feminine energy of Mother Earth continually recreates humanity's home. Bless her, and be grateful you are a woman.

To recapture the important points of the chapter:

1. Through reclaiming our sexuality, we reclaim our power and help to rebalance masculine and feminine energies on the planet.

2. Practice communicating about your female sexuality.

3. Learn to love your body as a beautiful expression of the feminine energy of nature.

4. Examine the messages of guilt and shame you have internalized through religious belief systems. Challenge these with a new understanding of women's true spiritual role.

5. Embrace the fire of the true virgin as you take back your sexual power.

PART TWO

Our Role in Our Families

About Part Two

In Part One, you began the process of healing your intimate relationships. Part Two of this book focuses on our role as women within the home and family. The Awakening chapter cites the abundance of research indicating that we women are overburdened in caring for our families and homes. It points out the many ways that we as women play a disproportionate role in the everyday task of keeping our households functioning, from housework to child care to caring for the elderly.

If you are single, you may still relate to the general pressures described in this chapter. If you're in a relationship with another woman, you may find that many of these dynamics apply for both of you. Again, focus on what feels relevant to your life, and skip over the rest.

The Solutions chapter of Part Two starts by exploring the implications on the economy of women's unpaid labor. By learning to value ourselves, our work, and our time, we take the first step towards reestablishing balance. This chapter helps us disentangle ourselves from the roles we play in fostering our family's dependence upon us, since we have been socialized to be codependent nurturers. Once we recognize this dynamic and how it operates, we can begin to set limits and allow other family members to take more responsibility for their own well-being and growth. This will free our time and energy both for ourselves and for a more active role in the world at large.

6

Awakening to Our Overburdened Roles in Our Home

Dishes to wash and spring to go,
Now I am married, I've everything to do.
When I was single, marryin' was my crave,
Now I'm married, I've troubles to my grave.

"FRONTIER SONGS," SINGLE GIRL

Woman's Work: In Our Home

In our homes, so many of us are lonely, overburdened caretakers.

In the subconscious mind of many women is the yearning to be taken care of. This is one of the reasons some of us marry. Because of our social conditioning, we come to fantasize being rescued from our parents, our job, or our life. It is ironic that once we marry we end up doing 75 percent of the household and caretaking chores, as well as going to work and contributing to our family's income.[1] We end up taking care of our husbands, our children, our older parents, our friends, and our animals. Then, for some strange reason, we can't figure out what's wrong in our lives—why we aren't happy or why we are so tired much of the time. There is not much left over for us.

Researchers have found that the greater the domestic burden at home for women, the lower the career status.[2] Domestic work also affects a woman's stress level. Married women tend to be more depressed, to experience poorer physical health, and to have lower self-esteem, especially in more traditional marital arrangements.[3]

When you read the following job description of a "homemaker," as defined by the New York state legislature, you can understand why depression sets in, and why our depression in marriage seems to be correlated with our roles in the relationship: "Homemakers are an unrecognized, unpaid part of the national work force, who make an invaluable contribution to the welfare and stability of the nation, but who receive no health, retirement or unemployment benefits."[4]

"A woman's work is never done" seems such an appropriate saying. Some 80 percent of the women in the United States now hold full- or part-time jobs.[5] If a woman has a job outside the home, her work is only two-thirds over after her workday ends. Once she arrives home, she is responsible for 74 to 92 percent of the work. She has the responsibility for grocery shopping, the errands, the meals, the laundry, the cleanup, and generally for tending to the needs, both emotional and physical, of the entire family. Full-time housewives average 8.1 hours per day in housework, while employed women average 4.8 hours per day in addition to their paying job. Yet husbands who also work full-time average only 1.6 hours per day in household chores.[6]

According to research on the division of household labor done by Arlie Hochschild, a sociology professor at the University of California, Berkeley, "Four out of five men do not share the work at home." You may be surprised to learn that "husbands of working wives spend no more time on housework than husbands of wives who do not work."[7] Most men do something, but they're less likely to do daily chores such as fixing breakfast or dinner. There is one exception: When a wife's salary competes with her husband's or she earns more, the husband usually helps more with the work in the home.[8] The balance of power seems to rest on the income produced, which is a good lesson for us.

So, you may say, why don't women ask our husbands to help? In many cases we do, and the most common result, according to researchers, is marital conflict and arguments.[9] Many women have found, whether they work outside the home or not, that it is very difficult to get men to help them with housework or child care. Men have been socialized to believe that household chores are "woman's work" and that it is a sign of weakness to be caught doing the housework. Housework is a major source of tension in most marriages, particularly when both partners work.

Even though many husbands give lip service to equality, we find that when men do chores in the home, they feel like they are helping with their wife's work. Even the kids "help Mommy" do her job. In fact, research shows that children tend to help women more than men with extra labor for household chores.[10] Neither husband nor children tend to help without some instruction or organization from the woman, which, once again, takes her time. Often women feel it is easier to do the chores themselves. When our husband does help, we women tend to express disproportionate gratitude. According to Dr. Hochschild, "we create myths about our husbands helping" more than they actually do to avoid conflict.

Now ask yourself, "Why am I so tired all the time?"

Caretaking

A woman is generally the emotional networker for the entire extended family as well, keeping in touch with both sides of the family, with her partner's parents and her own parents, with grandparents, and with other friends and relatives. We are the glue that bonds one generation to the other and keeps the family close. We do the arranging and planning for families to reunite during the holidays and other important family occasions. We keep generations, both young and old, linked together.

At some time in our life we are usually the major caretaker for one or more of our own or our spouse's elderly parents. Middle-aged women with children on the one end and elderly parents on the other end are under particular stress. According to the Older Women's League (OWL), an organization founded in 1980 that compiles statistics and prepares educational materials, the typical woman can expect to spend seventeen years caring for children and eighteen years caring for older family members while also being employed.[11] Caregiving for the elderly or sick often costs a woman many years of her own life.

A woman may spend sixty hours a week to provide physical and emotional support for a family of four. If she works a forty-hour-a-week job in addition, it's easy to see why she is so fatigued and stressed.

Children

Women have always held major responsibility for the care and nurturing of children, and even today the major portion of child care, both emotional and physical, is still handled by women. We receive only 20 percent input, help, or support from our partners in caring for our children.

This responsibility for the children is exacerbated when there is a divorce in the family. This is true for greater numbers of women. According to a study cited by David Blankenhorn, author of *Fatherless in America*, "In 1990 fathers were absent in 27.5 percent of all homes with mothers and children, up from 21.6 percent in 1979. Approximately ten million homes in 1990 consisted of mothers living with children whose fathers were absent."[12] Women are usually responsible for the raising of the children, even though statistics show that their finances may fall by 50 to 60 percent after a divorce. The percentage of men who don't pay child support outweighs the percentage who do. "Sixty to eighty percent of the children eligible for child support receive none," according to the Women's Legal Defense Fund.[13] A 1997 General Accounting Office report points out that four out of five delinquent parents—the vast majority of whom are men—still do not pay child support despite the efforts of the Clinton administration to help states collect the payments.[14] In most cases, the children end up being a major responsibility of the woman throughout her lifetime, whether she is married or divorced.

Some 70 percent of working mothers are employed full-time, with almost half of working women having children who are under the age of one.[15] Women may carry a great deal of guilt and conflict over their roles as mothers versus their work in outside jobs or careers. The good news for guilty working mothers is that even early studies have shown "that high achievement of mothers is even more predictive of high achievement of both their sons and their daughters than is the high achievement of fathers."[16] Researchers have also concluded that children of working mothers "develop more flexible and less stereotypic gender roles in dual-career families than in traditional families."[17]

There is no evidence that children of working mothers (as compared to mothers not employed outside the home) face any cognitive or emotional deficiencies, so working mothers can breathe a collective sigh of relief. These mothers also deserve some personal recognition for setting a positive role model that is achievement-oriented and healthy for their children.

To conclude, there is no doubt that women in general perform the lion's share of household chores. Our society has assigned us the major responsibility for children and older family members who need care. This affects us on every level of our lives, since the time and energy we put into housework or into nurturing others is time and energy we don't have to put into ourselves or our work on behalf of the planet.

7

Solutions Through Changing Our Roles

*The unpaid labor of women in the household,
if given economic value, would add an estimated
one-quarter to one-third, $8,000,000,000,000,
to the world's annual economic product.*

RUTH LEGER SIVARD, *Women: A World Survey,* 1996

How does all this unpaid labor, housework, child care, cooking, shopping, errand running, and so forth we women do affect our larger world? Why should we even worry about it, besides the fact, of course, that we are exhausted?

Let me explain the effect your work in the home has on the larger world around you. Let me show you how important you really are and how crucial it is to balance the sex roles in our culture so that women can have more time for input in the larger world. The world cannot change until we change ourselves.

Gender Balance

The continuing survival of life on our planet depends upon our ability to balance the dominating masculine energy with the feminine qualities of nurturing and connectedness. Although the current imbalance of gender energies is a global problem, its solution begins within our own families and our own homes.

Here in America it is widely acknowledged that the family structure is dysfunctional and lacking in balance. A large part of this dysfunction is caused by the gender role stereotypes that have been passed from generation to generation—the rather distant, breadwinning husband-father, and the nurturing, over-functioning and emotional wife-mother, who in our era is also a financial provider. Although she now works outside the home, the wife-mother does the majority of the unpaid work, which includes housekeeping, caretaking, and the development of others, including her husband. Housework and caretaking do have value, but not in a dysfunctional society. In a dysfunctional society, only money has value, along with power. Because it is unpaid, the woman's work in the home is considered valueless. In the meantime, the man gains importance in the outside world as he pursues his career with more freedom.

This model for the family structure clearly doesn't work. Children brought up under this paradigm have all suffered from the pain of low self-value for the female and the need for the male to be strong or macho. This structure has contributed to emotional starvation for the father and the devaluation of the mother, which they in turn recreate for their children. To change this pattern, we need to get in touch with our authenticity as human beings and set aside our gender roles.

We as women must boost our importance and worth in the family and home and at the same time increase the value of the home for men and enhance their nurturing qualities. When we accomplish this task, we can put an end to the unequal valuation of the two genders. We are called upon to create a new role model for women. We need to create an aura of power, value, and respect around womanhood. Until we have that power, value, and respect in the family, we will not be taken seriously in the world. Hence, we will not have the power to change the business and governmental structures. As John Kenneth Galbraith, the famous economist, wrote in his now-classic *Economics and Public Purpose,* "The household, in the established economics, is essentially a disguise for the exercise of male authority."[1]

Women's Free Labor: The Basis of the World Economy

Women's unpaid labor in the home, which includes housecleaning, laundry, caretaking, meal preparation, and caring for the young and the elderly, in essence subsidizes the major corporations, the higher echelons of the economy. This in turn gives them more financial assets and freedom to buy and irresponsibly use the Earth's natural resources.

How can doing the dishes support a patriarchal economy? Let me explain the basics.

1. Because women are assigned the housework and childrearing responsibilities, we are limited in our ability to compete with men or to have influence in the higher echelons of business and government where the major decisions about the planet are made.

2. Women are used as a reserve labor force, called out in times of labor shortages and then encouraged via the media, in times of labor surplus, to return to the home and domestic work. A prime example occurred during World War II. After being trained as welders, shipbuilders, and so forth during the war, women were discouraged from working after the war ended and encouraged to return to the home and stay there to raise the post-war Baby Boom generation. Hence the 1950s media image of a woman was that of a happy housewife and mother.

3. The unpaid labor of women makes the male employees more efficient executives or workers, since it frees men to concentrate on their jobs and career, while their environment, food, clothing, and children, the next labor force, are taken care of for free even if the wife works.

4. Women also provide emotional and psychological caretaking to men and create a safe buffer from the competitive workplace.

5. Women reproduce and socialize the next generation of labor for the economy. In addition, the housewife also provides the main support for consumerism, according to economist John Kenneth Galbraith, who says, "Idealizing women's roles as wives and mothers has been 'a convenient social virtue,' convenient for business and industry."[2]

In thinking about the American economy, imagine a five-layer cake. The bottom layer of the cake would be Mother Earth and her natural resources. The second layer, where women provide most of their free services, consists of unpaid household work, volunteer work, parenting, caring for the young, sick, and elderly, and other caretaking. The third layer is made up of the public sector, including local, state, and federal government and the corresponding infrastructure. The fourth layer of the cake is the working sector—employees, small and medium-sized businesses, investment, and production. The fifth layer is the private sector of the economy where corporations rule. This is the richest part of the cake, and the heads of these corporations are the wealthiest. They develop their wealth by utilizing the energies of the lower four layers of the economy cake. The bottom two layers are based on the feminine energies of resources and unpaid labor. The top layers tend to be dominated by masculine energies.[3]

The current economic structure does not value the contributions of women. To add insult to injury, the years of being a housewife are called "zero years" by the Social Security Administration. Housewives receive no pension. There is no other occupation or career that includes so much work for others with no pay and no retirement benefits, and whose skills are less valued than that of the housewife, who may be working as well in the business world.

If our male partners keep us busy cleaning up after them and maintaining their home environment for them, the larger environment will continue to be destroyed for our own children and for generations to come. For it is the nurturing, other-directed, connected female energy that is needed out in today's world to balance the hierarchical, material, competitive, territorial corporate energy that shows no respect for the planet's resources and delicate ecosystems.

Studies reveal that when women have resources or make money, children's nutritional level and well-being improve greatly.[4] In other words, when women have power, the children benefit and I believe it is fair to say the Earth will benefit. An often-cited United Nations report claims that women "do two-thirds of the world's work, receive 10 percent of the income, and own 1 percent of the property."[5] While women bear most of the responsibility, men hold most of the power. Women's responsibility includes work both inside and outside the home, and caring for others' welfare within the family. The imbalance in power and responsibility filters directly into the family and home, and provides an obvious foundation for a dysfunctional family—a family in which there is much less power, respect, and value for women than there is for men.

We Need a Better System

Tradition and fear of change have kept the belief systems around women's roles very similar over hundreds of years.

We now need to look for a better system than sexism to determine human roles and values. Women can't go on being the supportive backbone of the family and the extended family, as well as the housekeeper, the one to care for the emotional needs of everyone, the physical and emotional caregiver to children, the errand woman, the shopper, the household financial accountant, and the career woman. We are killing ourselves and our enjoyment of life. We are called upon as women to change the role of men as well as our own role towards a fairer distribution of labor.

And while women are kept busy in a smaller environment, the resources and environment of Mother Earth are being destroyed. We have to reevaluate our situation and our priorities and take a global perspective of women's and men's roles.

Dysfunctional for Planet Earth

Women's free labor expands corporate and governmental systems, which uses the Earth's natural resources as the basis of most of their products. Although unpaid work and the exploitation of resources do fuel a profitable economy, the present system causes the pollution and degradation of our oceans, our atmosphere, and our Earth. This is *not profitable* for the feminine energies or for us as women.

There are many ways to look at how women's unpaid labor affects the world. Marilyn Waring, in her book *If Women Counted,* explains: "The treatment of women and children in the system of natural accounts have many fundamental parallels."[6] Charlotte O'Kelly, a professor of sociology, and Larry Carney, a teacher of comparative international development, write that the roles of the full-time housewife and full-time breadwinner are very dysfunctional for our planet, since they contribute both to problems of overpopulation and a burgeoning, materialistic consumerism that burdens our limited global resources.[7]

We can begin to see how the extreme gender roles we act out in our daily lives create dysfunction in our relationships, in our families, and on our Earth. As women, we can begin to balance these roles. When you think that you are not important the next time you do your husband's laundry, think twice. You are very important! Your housework and caretaking affect the entire world, for better or for worse. You have an impact not only on your family and your children, but on future generations who will model their family roles after your family, either freeing themselves or keeping the energy of women trapped.

You are affecting women's role in the workplace and the business community, where without the help of male participation in the home, women will always have to struggle to stay even.

You are affecting the oceans and the Earth and the atmosphere around it because women's free labor, along with the Earth's natural resources, is the basis for all production in an industrial society.[8] Do you even begin to recognize the power we women have? What if we stopped performing our unpaid work?

Awakening to our power is like throwing a pebble into a still lake. Waves or vibrations ripple from it. Decide how you want to contribute to saving our planet and our future. Begin by changing the dysfunctional and valueless role we women have been playing. Begin in your homes and with your family.

External Solutions: Women's Role in the Family

Men overwhelm women with their physical needs.

In comparison studies, research has shown that a single woman with the same size family as that of a married woman will actually spend less time on housework. Why? Because studies show what we have all suspected: "Husbands may require more housework than they contribute."[9]

If women overfunction, men will definitely underfunction in housework, because from a man's point of view, housework carries neither status nor value. Yet, when housework is paid for, it amounts to a valuable commodity. A 1976 study estimated the economic value of a year of housework to be $13,000. At 1990 rates, it was around $25,000 a year.[10] As we approach the year 2000, it will be even more. When we factor in that employed wives usually provide over 40 percent of the family's financial income,[11] and add to our salary $25,000 to $30,000, then we begin to see how much we are really worth in the marketplace!

Finally, as if to justify our housecleaning role, women have been living under the myth that doing the housework and taking care of another person's dirt means "I love you." This myth, which has been enhanced by the media, dictates that washing a man's dirty underwear and erasing the ring around his collar is the best way of saying "I love you." If this is true, then why don't more men do housework to let us women know they love us?

QUEEN OR DOORMAT?

The solution to dispelling the degrading myth of women earning love through housework is simple. Pablo Picasso once expressed it eloquently when he said, "There are two kinds of women in this world: Queens and Doormats!" Consider the following.

Women feel inferior and lose self-esteem because we perform devalued work; we have allowed ourselves to become Doormats. Start by letting your partner wash his own dirty underwear. Show him you love him not by being his servant but by giving him a hug and a kiss and saying the actual words: "I love you." Be your man's queen, not his servant. You'll both be happier. I have never heard a man say he was attracted to the woman who does the TV "collar commercials" for detergent. Instead, try being a queen like Julia Roberts or Elizabeth Taylor. You don't see them doing laundry on television! Do you get the point? Simply put, it is time we elevated our status in our homes. And this begins by changing our role from the bottom of the laundry basket up.

Changing Our Roles in the Family

Currently, many of us are trying to fulfill both the past traditional role of housewife, mother, caretaker, and the role of financial provider, worker, professional, and career woman outside the home. Most of us have nothing left over for ourselves except exhaustion. If we are to survive, we are called upon to change ourselves and our roles within our family.

Why is yet another burden, the burden of change, placed on us? Because by and large men will not voluntarily offer to "take less" or "give more." Women must initiate the changes. And after a little turbulence, our families will adjust to our new roles. In fact, in many instances, our family members will blossom into healthier individuals, united and working together, instead of one individual doing it all and *enabling* others not to take care of themselves. To begin, let's examine our current role within the family unit.

The role of caregiver is usually required of women in our culture. We are taught to be other-directed and more vigilant to others' needs than to our own. While concern for others is a valuable quality, within our culture caretaking is a subordinate role, a role for which women, not men, are socialized. We are socialized for this subordinate role from the time we are children.

If we are to balance the male-female roles in our dysfunctional families, we must begin by balancing our own energy output in the home. We can change our roles by changing the feminine behavior of overfunctioning.

Changing Our Role in the Home

How do we as women change our role in the home? It is actually very simple. First, we need to stop overfunctioning for others and let them learn to function for themselves up to their age and developmental capacity. If you are overfunctioning in a relationship or in your family by doing most of the housework and caretaking, you can count on the reality that you are enabling others to underfunction. If you are overresponsible for others, you are being less than responsible for yourself. Simply stop doing it all, and learn to delegate responsibility. You can accomplish this one responsibility at a time.

Every good corporate leader knows the vital importance of delegating responsibilities or tasks to another individual. Corporate executives know that their time is valuable. So why do women try to do it all in the home? Does all the housework really belong to us? Is it really *all* our job? Of course it isn't! The model of women overworking is extremely outrageous, particularly when we consider today's economic demands of dual-income households. Like corporate executives, we need to value our time and energy.

DELEGATING HOUSEWORK

To begin to learn how to delegate housework, you can take the following simple steps:

1. First, know you are a valuable person and develop the self-esteem to realize that your time is of utmost im-

portance. Time is like money, and how you spend your time is important. If you live to be eighty-two years old, there will be almost 30,000 days in your life. How many days do you think you have left? How do you want to spend them? After all, this is your life "time."

2. Decide to delegate one task at a time to another person. Don't overwhelm your partner, your family members, or yourself by delegating everything at once. If you do, you will meet with anger and resistance. To be successful, you do best to approach change slowly and with positive reinforcement.

3. Begin determining whose responsibility a task might really be. Write a list. Whose laundry or room are you cleaning? Is the person capable of doing the task her- or himself? You wouldn't ask a four-year-old to do his or her own laundry, but you could ask your husband to do his and to help do his share of the children's.

4. When asking others to do specific tasks, it is important to make them feel good about taking on the responsibility. With a husband and children, you can explain that it will mean more quality and fun time together if the housework is shared and everyone works together as a team.

5. In a positive way, write a description of exactly what the job is, when it is to be done, how often, and how to do it. Always talk about the rewards the sharing will offer to both or all of you. Help your partner or family to see how valuable the task is to living comfortably in the home.

When delegating household responsibilities, it is important to teach other family members how valuable work in the home can be and how important the person is who does the work. This is a good reminder of your own importance! The sharing of household responsibilities creates your environment, as well as a certain lifestyle for your whole family to use as a launching point into the outside world. It also teaches your family that it is not just one person's responsibility to make the home environment comfortable. Modeling shared responsibility helps change the world by giving a new generation a more positive guidepost. Housework is a team effort, just like tasks at the office, at school, or at play that make relationships more successful. Explain to your family that the sharing of physical tasks will balance the emotional relationships and rid the family of unnecessary resentments and tensions.

Men and Helping Behavior

In her book *You Just Don't Understand,* Deborah Tannen explained that "many women are inclined to do what is asked of them and many men are inclined to resist even the slightest hint that anyone, especially a woman, is telling them what to do." So the woman will repeat the request and the male will again put it off—nagging then becomes the result.[12]

But when do men like to help? Research has shown that men like to help when it might be heroic or chivalrous, if the help will be observed by others, or if it might be dangerous.[13] In other words, the bottom line in soliciting a man's help requires boosting his ego or making him feel like a hero. Use this knowledge as you delegate your housework, and don't let yourself fall back into old patterns of trying to do it all yourself. Ask yourself: Who appointed toilet cleaning to be a woman's job? The answer is, those who didn't want to do it themselves. But now that we are sharing the role of provider for the family, they need to help us in our old assigned role of house cleaner.

Inner Solutions: With Love, Set Your Boundaries

The author Vernon Howard tells us to "peer closely at the faces and lives of 'yes' people. What do you see? You see pathetic men and women who have agreed to their own defeat. They have meekly and foolishly surrendered to a life of exhaustion, chaos, and futility." Howard goes on to observe that "people want your 'yes' as a first step towards getting whatever else they want from you. This is a plain fact and those who choose to ignore it will remain as victims."[14]

We as women have allowed ourselves to be "yes people" for too long. We need to let go of needing outside approval, because this keeps us constantly other-directed instead of centered in our own strengths. What others think of us will always vary, no matter how much we try to do for them. Pleasing behavior will always create anxiety within. Women put enough energy outward towards others. We need to learn to be loved for who we are, not for what we do for others. It is now time for us to "just say no" with ease and without fear.

When you say no, you can do it gently, and after you say no, just be silent. Don't back-pedal or give excuses, as so many of us do to avoid hurting another's feelings. You aren't required to give explanations. "No" is all you need to say.

Codependence and Women

Codependence is just another word for how we women are socialized. We are taught to be vigilant to, in tune with, and to overfunction for others, especially in our family. But we are not taught to be respectful of our own needs. This enables others to refuse responsibility for themselves or their actions, as we dance to the codependent shuffle of "Give, give, give, resent! Give, give, give, resent!"

To determine if you are behaving codependently, ask yourself what kind of covert sense of power, manipulation, control, or accomplishment you get from doing or being everything to everybody. Do you feel like a martyr? Codependent behavior, which results in feelings of martyrdom, actually makes others feel guilty and distances them emotionally from us. It is self-indulgent, self-pitying behavior.

There is a difference between being supportive and trying to meet everyone's emotional needs. Emotional caregiving can involve padding others' lives emotionally, and trying never to hurt another person's feelings. Yet each of us, adult or child, learns from our emotional experiences, both painful and joyous, in life. Painful experiences can help mold people into great human beings. We can learn to allow another person's emotional pain to happen while being supportive. We do not have the power to take everyone's emotional pain away—whether it be our elderly parent's or our child's. And why should we? It might be the motivation for their success or their growth! Your loved ones learn invaluable lessons from suffering the consequences of their behavior and overcoming their own emotional problems. This is known as learning coping mechanisms.

To gauge your emotional caretaking barometer, ask yourself how much of yourself you have to give away to feel loved. Is it 70 percent, 80 percent, or 90 percent? Take the steps to change the percentage. Learn to be supportive and lovingly detached as you let others live and experience their own lives. Steps to facilitate this change might include attending CODA (Codependents Anonymous) meetings or working with a good therapist.

As we near the new millennium, we are called upon to let go of our socialized self-sacrificing roles and learn to live in joy ourselves, and enjoy our family and our life.

Change Takes Time

It is quite normal for any system or family to resist change, particularly when that change increases their responsibility for themselves. So as you say no and stop overfunctioning for others, they may gripe, refuse to do, throw tantrums, sulk, manipulate— anything to get you to return to your old behavior, which they are used to. Just allow it, and hold the course. It's only an adjustment period.

To get through this adjustment period, keep telling your family, husband, partner, and kids, "I love you, but I have been enabling you to be irresponsible, and that has not been good for either you or for me." Just keep repeating this in an even tone of voice and stay centered. You might want to focus your energy in your womb as you learned in the centering exercise in Part One. Don't let your family's antics against change throw you off center. Take a deep breath. The house might even be a mess for a while. This is not the end of the world! Don't get obsessive and step in to do it yourself again. Change takes time for adjustment by all of you, and undoubtedly you will be tested. Think of the mess as an investment in your future, your family's future responsibility, and your family's future happiness. When you feel wobbly about the changes you're making, you might remember the following:

To Let Go

To let go is not to stop caring.
It's recognizing I can't do it for someone else.
To let go is not to cut myself off.
It's realizing I can't control another.

To let go is not to enable,
But to allow learning from natural consequences.
To let go is not to fight powerlessness,
But to accept that the outcome is not in my hands.

To let go is not to try to change or blame others.
It's to make the most of myself.
To let go is not to care for; it's to care about.
To let go is not to fix; it's to be supportive.

To let go is not to judge.
It's to allow another to be a human being.
To let go is not to try to arrange outcomes,
But to allow others to affect their own destinies.

To let go is not to be protective.
It's to permit others to face their own reality.
To let go is not to regulate anyone,
but to strive to become what I dream I can be.

To let go is not to fear less; it's to love more.

ANONYMOUS

To conclude, it is time for us women to reorganize our roles in the family structure that support the male and his career and fail to support the woman.

Men will have to change, for we need to equalize and share both the benefits and the burden of the income women earn working outside the home—including the extra housework, child care, and so on that we no longer have time for. After all, if wives didn't work, 60 percent of families in the United States would fall below the poverty line.[15] The problem begins at home. Is our time valuable? Yes. Are we valuable? Yes. Isn't the Earth worth the effort of making the change?

To recapture the important points of this chapter:

1. Begin to acknowledge the dysfunctional nature of the typical family structure in which the woman does the lion's share of the work. Women's unpaid labor supports a patriarchal economy, including disrespect of the environment.

2. Learn to say "I love you" directly rather than through performing a disproportionate amount of the housework and child care. Be a Queen, not a Doormat.

3. Stop overfunctioning and enabling others to underfunction. Change your role in the home by learning to delegate, one task at a time.

4. Set your boundaries and learn to say no when appropriate. Overcome codependence.

5. Recognize your true value and act accordingly. The future of the Earth depends upon it.

The Reality of Our Lives in the Workplace

About Part Three

In Parts One and Two, you explored your life at home, in terms of relationships and your role in the family. I hope you are feeling more empowered and beginning to truly appreciate your worth as a woman. Part Three of this book focuses on women's role as income earners. The Awakening chapters illustrate the current economic realities that keep women disenfranchised within the workforce. Women typically earn less money than men for the same work, and women also tend to be concentrated in lower-paying sectors of the job market. In addition, complex social structures keep women in subordinate positions. Whether we're self-employed or working in a corporate job, we all pay the price for how women as a whole are treated.

The Solutions chapters teach women to begin balancing our role in the workplace by contacting our own inner feminine power. Key lessons are presented which can help us increase our sense of authority, mobilize our creativity, and show us how to manifest our career goals. After we practice these exercises of inner empowerment, we can fruitfully engage in external actions to combat stereotypes and break through the "glass ceiling." We can organize "circles of women" and perform other "matriarchal tasks" to enable us to work together on strategies to create real changes in the workplace, including the possibility of starting our own business. By creating this solid base in our work life, we will have the resources and energy needed to help us take action in the larger world to affect the lives of women everywhere and the ultimate fate of the planet.

8

Awakening to Realities of Our Place in the Business World

Of one thing I am sure, however. There will be no real content among American women unless they are made and kept more ignorant or unless they are given equal opportunity with men to use what they have been taught. And American men will not really be happy until their women are.

PEARL S. BUCK

The Smithsonian National Museum of American History had an exhibit on women's jobs in industrial America that included advertisements for women's jobs from the 1800s. Some of the ads read: "That particular dexterity, patience, and forbearance possessed by the average woman in a degree superior to that of the opposite sex" (the Telephone Company); "For their dexterity and carefulness" (a Civil War gun manufacturer which assigned women the more dangerous job of loading powder). One watch company boasted that "one girl at $8.00 a week could do the work of four men formerly employed at $25.00 each." As exhibit coordinator Deborah Warner revealed, "No matter what job they performed, women were paid women's wages, which were generally less than half as much as men in comparable situations could expect." In addition, women's jobs were stagnant, with almost no promise for upward mobility. Even educated women were pigeonholed for life into teaching jobs, secretarial positions, or work as librarians.[1]

In nineteenth-century America, money truly became the standard measure of a person's worth. Work done for "free," such as housework by wives, carried low value and status.[2] Today, being a housewife in our society still carries low value and low pay. In fact, "For women, marriage is no longer a stable, rewarding, lifetime career," according to R. Davis, professor emeritus at the University of Southern California, and coauthor P. Vanden Oever of an article entitled "Demographic Foundations of New Sex Roles."[3] The research indicates that "women's prospects are that around two-thirds of their adult years will be spent without children in the household, and possibly half to two-thirds without a husband. For long periods, women will probably be thrown on their own resources and will need employment." That means that for our very survival, women in today's society must be aware of our employment status, opportunities, and what is happening in business with regard to attitudes towards women. Women's participation in the paid work market also provides the independence for us to make choices in our lives, such as choices to delay marriage or to dissolve marriages that are abusive for ourselves or our children. Careers increase women's freedom from domination and also influence how much power we are given in the world. The higher we are on the ladder, the more impact we will have on the decisions relating to the Earth's resources and the environment. So where do women actually stand today in the world of work outside the home?

Women in the Business World

We exchange our time in our life for money through our work. Are women getting a fair rate of exchange? According to *Fortune* magazine, things have changed since the 1900s, but women of the twentieth century still do not rank among America's top executives in any significant numbers. By the year 2005, women will make up about half of the full-time labor force, but it won't be the top half.[4] As *Fortune* pointed out, "The cool reception that women once got at the door has followed them up the organizational hierarchy. For all but an exceptional few, the corner office still looks as remote as it did to Rosie the Riveter."[5] In its 1990 survey of the 4,012 highest paid officers and directors of the top 799 top public companies, *Fortune* found that only 19 were women, which is less than one-half of 1 percent. In addition, a poll of CEOs found that nearly 81 percent acknowledged discrimination against women in the workplace, with stereotyping of women and preconceptions of female behavior listed as the reasons for this discrimination.

While women are indeed being promoted, this is only taking place up to a certain level, and then we seem to hit a "ceiling" that prevents us from going further. Because of this invisible and unacknowledged discrimination and gender bias when it comes to promotions, males are picked over females for key executive or managerial positions. Less than 3 percent to 5 percent of senior executive positions are held by women.[6] In our federal government, women make up only 13 percent of the executives, but 72 percent of the bottom ranks of federal workers. Of the employees who make the minimum wage or below, 62 percent are women.[7] In the 1990s women are 43 percent of the work force in administrative and managerial occupations but earn only 67 percent as much as their male counterparts.[8]

According to Dr. F. Crosby of Smith College and other researchers, both women and men are aware of workplace discrimination, but most women do not realize there is a good chance it is happening directly to them.[9] In fact, you might want to take a moment to reevaluate your own work situation.

A notable example of the toll sexism takes on a woman was that of Dr. Frances R. Conley, a full-tenured professor of neurosurgery at Stanford University Medical School, who made headlines in 1991 by resigning from Stanford with this statement to the media: "I resigned because of a subtle sexism that, while not physically harmful, is extremely pervasive and debilitating." Conley said she "was tired of being treated as less than an equal person, of being condescendingly called 'Hon' by my peers, of having my honest differences of opinion put down as a manifestation of premenstrual syndrome, of having my ideas treated less seriously than those of the men with whom I work. I wanted my dignity back."[10]

Sexism not only affects the quality of our everyday working lives but also our long-term goals and our future monetary lifestyle. Ten years after graduation, a female college graduate with the same or better credentials as a man will be in a lower position and only making three-fourths of what a male would make at that same position. Some 70 percent of the 57 million women working in the business world still made less than $20,000 a year in 1994.[11]

The Pink-Collar Ghetto and Limited Opportunities

Are you in a "pink-collar job"? According to the Department of Labor, women are still concentrated in lower-paying occupations where they earn about three-fourths what men do for the same work.[12] Pink-collar jobs, as they are called, are those in which at least 60 percent or more of the job holders are women.

These jobs typically support the male professionals, and in most cases provide a tremendous amount of the man's work. They are dead-end jobs that are segregated and pay only a fraction of what the men we work for are earning.

Many pink-collar jobs involve a great deal of stress due to the high demand and low control aspects of the job, a combination that is particularly stressful.[13] As of 1995, 98.5 percent of the secretaries in the United States were women, 92.8 percent of the bookkeepers, 84.1 percent of the elementary school teachers, 79.2 percent of the cashiers, and 81.7 percent of the office clerks.[14] Dental assistants, receptionists, data entry keyers, librarians, and bank tellers are all female-intensive, pink-collar positions. This segregated situation limits our work options as women and also contributes to gender gap wages, which means the higher the percentage of women in an occupation, the lower the pay. Susan Faludi, in her book *Backlash,* researched data from the Bureau of Labor Statistics and concluded: "As much as 45 percent of the pay gap is caused by sex segregation in the work force." Job discrimination and segregation by sex role maintains male power and the lower status of women in the workplace.[15]

Women generally have more years of schooling than men, but today women make only 75 cents to every dollar a man makes.[16] Research by the Institute for Women's Policy Research indicates that "only half of this reduction in the wage gap was the result of an increase in women's real wages; the other half reflected a decline in men's salaries."[17] While this wage gap has been shrinking, it has shrunk by only a penny every year. "[T]here has been progress since the days when women earned 59 cents for every dollar men earned. At the rate we are going, we'll close the pay gap by 2025 or so, and we won't close the representation gap [of women in executive positions] for more than 400 years."[18] Just as depressing, about 70 percent of us currently *make less* than $20,000 a year. Only about 11 percent of women make over $30,000 a year.[19] It's only natural that a survey released by the American Federation of Labor and Congress of Industrial Organizations in the fall of 1997 revealed that equal pay for equal work is the top concern of working women.[20]

Unequal Pay:
Economic Dependence on Men Is the Consequence

The consequence of this wage inequality is to keep women economically and psychologically dependent upon men for a decent lifestyle. This vicious cycle leads to our hoping to be freed from our dead-end, low-paying job by meeting Prince Charming, because we can't make enough money as a woman to support ourselves or our children in a middle-class lifestyle. We have to look for and towards a man for our financial security, because generally men are the ones in our society who make the most money and have the better job.

The huge sums of money that certain privileged men can make was headlined in a *Los Angeles Times* article that declared: "U.S. executives are among the most highly paid in the world." As the article pointed out, in 1991 a $75.1 million salary was paid to Anthony O'Reilly, CEO of H. J. Heinz; a $34.6 million salary to Martin Wygod of Medco Containment; and a $23.3 million salary was paid to John C. Malone of Tele-Communications."[21] Even the severance pay of CEOs is astronomical. An article in the *New York Times,* "Giant Payoffs for Executives Who Fail Big," points out that failure for CEOs pays. John R. Walter left AT&T in July 1997 with nearly a $26 million settlement. Michael Ovitz spent 14 months at the Walt Disney Company and received $90 million; Gilbert Amelio got at least $7 million from Apple Computer in July 1997; and Robert F. Greenhill left the Smith Barney division of Travelers Group less than three years after joining it in 1993 and collected $22 million.[22]

A *Forbes* magazine survey reported that in the five years from 1986 to 1991, a total of $1.1 billion in salaries was paid to 25 chief executives. In addition, out of the 800 largest companies, another 407 male executives made over $1 million each. In 1994, 187 to 1 was the ratio between the highest ranking executive's salary and the average company worker's salary. That means they made $187 for every $1 their workers made. This is clearly the mark of greed, and it's getting worse.[23]

The hidden headline, however, is that the majority of the poor in America are women and children. Women's poverty is due in part to the male-female wage gap for equivalent work. The average yearly income of women workers in 1992 was $11,046.[24] The second reason for female poverty is limited opportunities for women in the workplace. With women working in lower-paying jobs and receiving only three-quarters of men's compensation, it is no surprise that at all age groups more adult women than men are living below the poverty level.

Single Mothers, Unequal Wages, and Poverty

The result of this wage and job discrimination is the high poverty level of women and children in our country. In fact, 35 percent of households headed by single and divorced mothers are at or below the poverty line. Of the 14 million families headed by women, 34.6 percent were below the poverty level in 1994.[25]

Many female heads of household never receive court-ordered child support from ex-husbands. Statistics show that only half the amount awarded for child support is ever paid, and the average child support was only $57.59 per week according to a *Newsweek* story in 1992.[26] Who can feed a child a healthy diet on $57.59 a week, let alone pay for the child's clothing, health care, and education? Once again, women were and are expected to be miracle workers.

So before you even have children, it might be wise to think twice. In all probability they will be your sole responsibility, whether you are married or divorced. And the research shows you can't count on much male support either financially or emotionally after a divorce. You also won't find support from the corporation you work for or the government you pay taxes to, all run by male-dominated energy.

This is why child support laws and enforcement are key for keeping women and children out of poverty and sustaining middle-class living standards. In addition, equal wages and opportunity for women along with day-care facilities are vitally important to helping single mothers and their children survive.

Older Women and the Workforce

The situation doesn't get any better as women age. According to the statistics prepared by the Older Women's League (OWL) for the Senate Special Committee on Aging, older women who seek to enter or remain in the workforce are subject to discrimination. In fact, there is double discrimination: first as a woman, second as an older person. In addition, during a recession, older women tend to be the first laid off. There is a double standard of aging in this country. Women become invisible with less power, while men have the potential to become more powerful.

As we know, there are three things in life that are certain: death, taxes, and aging. Although most younger women are in denial that aging will happen to them, the majority of us will be older women. In America today there are 46.8 million mid-life and older women. Almost 60 percent of women over sixty-five are widowed and live alone.[27] Older women in our culture are treated as the most disposable. Most have reared their children, nourished their husbands and families, and worked outside the home, but they are still depreciated. Our society values women for their youth and beauty, and not enough for their wisdom.

In matriarchal cultures, older women are looked up to as mentors, rulers, and role models. An older woman has power. She is the majority on some governing councils, including those of the Cherokee nation. The Cherokees say governing women will weigh more heavily the decision of war, for they send their husbands and sons into death. Women provide the balance for male aggression.

The United States is the richest country on Earth, and yet the mothers of America, the elderly women, are one of the poorest groups in the nation. They are twice as likely as men to have incomes below the poverty line. Their average income in 1993 was $8,499; some 77.5 percent of women sixty-five and over had incomes below $15,000 a year.[28] In our retirement, we women have a 60 percent chance of being poor because the jobs that women hold rarely qualify them for private pensions. Only 18 percent of older women collect private pensions.[29]

And if you are planning to retire, don't plan on retiring early if you are a woman. A University of Miami study done on early retirement and gender found that although "the numbers of working men and women aged 40 to 60 are nearly equal, three-fourths of early retirees are men."[30] Labor force participation for women aged 55 to 64 was 49.2 percent in 1995, compared with 27 percent of women in 1950.[31] The conclusion is that women cannot afford to retire early, because they have not made enough to save or invest for an early retirement.

Another common problem is that many women who have been mothers and full-time housewives find themselves abandoned in their fifties or sixties through divorce or death, leaving them with no business experience. These women are terrified, and with good reason.

Thus, the mothers idealized in our American myths are actually abused, left in poverty, and abandoned in great numbers as we get older. Our society and the workplace are hostile to us. As mentioned earlier, the years a mother might take off work to have a child or care for her family are called "zero years" by the Social Security Administration, meaning they carry no monetary benefits. This shows how little value our society places on women's work within the home and family.

With so little power, how can we expect to be a force for positive change in the corporate world? We are called upon to increase our strength, our positions, and our value so that we can influence and integrate into a masculine sector that is currently playing a chief role in destroying our Earth.

9

Awakening to Jobs, Power, and Social Structure

*If woman were not bodily and mentally weak,
she would be extremely dangerous.*

DR. MOEBIUS,
Treatise on the Imbecility of Women, 1901

Economics and Social Structure

It is important to understand why women are so undervalued in the economic sphere. If we look at our social structure in the United States, we will find the answers to why women have had limited opportunities and unequal pay in the workplace.

In almost all social structures, people are ranked by power and by status. As social scientists such as Dr. Jean Baker-Miller explain, our American culture is basically divided into two categories: the dominant and the subordinate.[1] The dominant group holds the power and chooses the jobs of power; the subordinate group is assigned lower jobs, which usually involve supporting the dominants. And, naturally, the majority of these jobs are tasks the dominants don't want to do. After all, the dominants are very possessive and protective of their positions of power and status, which they usually compete only with each other for, and they tell the subordinates that they are not smart enough to hold these positions. The dominant group usually tries to block the progress, development, and freedom of the subordinate groups, whose energy and time are kept busy in survival mode. Thus, the subordinate groups have neither the time nor the energy to rebel.

> *There are villages in which men fish and women weave,*
> *and those in which women fish and men weave, but in*
> *either type of village, the work done by men is valued*
> *higher than the work done by women.*
>
> MARGARET MEAD

White males make up 29 percent of the workforce yet hold 95 out of 100 senior management positions in America. Women hold fewer than 5 percent of senior management positions. The reasons, concluded the "glass ceiling commission" initiated by the Department of Labor, is that white males' fear and anger leads them to thwart the progress of women and minorities.[2]

Because dominants hold and guard the power among themselves, they are seen as superior and more valuable in our society than the subordinates. Subordinates compete for relationships with dominants because they can give status and economic stability to a subordinate's life in accordance with how much power they have.

Subordinates are encouraged to please the dominant group, both visually, physically, and psychologically. Subordinates are not allowed to display anger or aggression; if they do, they are threatened, ostracized, or ridiculed. If subordinates rebel, they are made to feel guilt, blame, and shame for not following the character traits of their role. The sad part is that many subordinates do not get angry because they believe the rules and the world are as the dominants have taught them. Some never wake up, and some subordinates just give up. A clear example of how dominants attempt to keep subordinates down is the use of the term *feminazi,* which is used against women who work for women's rights. The dominant group will be hostile towards any subordinates who try to change their status.

Sociologists use a term called *ascription* to describe the fact that a person becomes unequal just by being born into a certain group and labeled from birth as a subordinate. That person is treated differently and taught differently.[3] In fact, the less educated the parents are, the more likely they are to encourage stereotypic sex-role behavior on the part of their children. As to who belongs to which group in America, you may have guessed by now that white males have been the dominant group, while women and other races have been the subordinates. This social gender set-up was observed by Alexis de Tocqueville as early as 1834: "In no country has such constant care been taken as in America to trace two clearly distinct lines of action for the two sexes, and to make them keep pace with the other, but in two pathways which are always different."[4]

In the early 1900s, the renowned student of Freud, psychiatrist Alfred Adler, talked about the fact that power and economics have influenced the division of labor in the United States by reserving the better positions for individuals of certain classes or sex. He said women are "allowed" activities in support of the male—activities that the male advantageously avoids. Adler found this structure to cause physical disturbance within the culture. In today's terms, this structure contributes to a dysfunctional society with tension between the sexes and the races. The top jobs are coveted by the dominants, who are very threatened and fearful, which turns into aggression when the status quo is questioned. Battles over affirmative action in the late 1990s reflect this fear and aggression. Adler goes on to state that this setup artificially nourishes delusions of grandeur in the male and feelings of inferiority in the female. He wrote that women learned from birth to undervalue themselves and their capabilities, thereby causing an imbalance in society.[5]

From relationships, to the home, to the workplace, this imbalance creates a dysfunction in our society, and most women have taken this social imbalance as normal. Many of us have a "patriarchal consciousness" rather than a *feminist* consciousness. The word *feminist* is not the dirty, nasty word some in the 1990s have made it out to be. It means simply to support the feminine, just as the word *patriotic* means to support the patriarchy.

We need to learn about our social structures so we can change them.

In implementing the changes we are called upon to make, we are bound to meet with resistance. As Cynthia Fuchs Epstein pointed out, "Gender distinctions are a basic element in the creation of the social order—and because those distinctions are typically stratified, with men at higher ranks—men have a stake in justifying and continuing the status quo. Challenges to a social order do not typically come from those that benefit from its arrangements."

It falls upon women and other subordinate groups to change this structure since it has definitely not been economically advantageous for us in the home, in the workplace, or in the world. The current social structure leaves us dependent and fearful, even if we do work outside the home and provide for ourselves and our children. It puts us in fear of our partner abandoning us, and it leaves many of us in poverty. For many older women, it means poverty if the dominant partner should walk out or die. We are always in struggle and survival mode.

In addition, this current social structure puts only one group in the position of making decisions for a diverse whole, allowing very little room for diversity or differences of the whole. From the Native Americans to the Latin Americans to the African Americans to women, we need room to grow into decision-making positions. We need to be free to live up to our own potentials, not tripped before the finish line by a big unseen foot.

Women of all groups need to connect for the common goal of equality, because many subordinates together equals more power than any dominant group. The old saying "Divide and conquer" has stood at the center of patriarchal consciousness. Let's join together for freedom, equality, and a healthier planet.

> *Culture can also behave like a healthy, open,*
> *and flexible personality that accommodates and*
> *assimilates new information, events, people, feelings,*
> *and thoughts, so that consciousness can expand and*
> *grow (though not without resistance to change).*
> *Times of transition are bumpy times, filled with*
> *ambivalence, dissatisfaction, uncertainty of direction,*
> *moments of truth, and decisions to make. This is so*
> *for institutions, organizations, and businesses*
> *as well as for cultures and individuals.*
>
> JEAN SHINODA BOLEN, *Ring of Power*

Bringing about a transition to the world envisioned by Bolen—and bringing our diverse and cooperative ideas into the decisions of our corporations and boardrooms—just might save our planet. But how can we create the upward path for women? The solutions lie within each one of us changing our stereotypic gender roles, connecting with one another, and assuming our responsibility and authority in the home and the workplace. Women also have a tremendous power as consumers, which we need to learn about and exercise wisely, with respect for the Earth's limited resources. It must be our vision to change the business environment before it is too late, since corporations have a major impact on our planet.

An interesting article entitled "In Praise of Female Strategy" appeared in *EuroBusiness* magazine applauding the cooperative and nurturing nature of women in the business world. It spoke of women's consensual style of "we" thinking instead of the masculine, military, confrontational "I" style of much of American business. The article concluded, "We are learning that there is not just another, but also a more effective way of doing business."[7]

10

Inner Solutions Through Taking Our Feminine Power

Within every woman there is a wild and natural creature,
a powerful force, filled with good instincts, passionate
creativity and ageless knowing.

CLARISSA PINKOLA ESTES,
Women Who Run With the Wolves

Taking our power in the workplace is so crucial that I will be devoting two chapters to the subject. There are four inner aspects that women need to develop to combat stereotypes of weakness and become successful in the workplace and the business world—and to position ourselves to facilitate change in the world at large. The four aspects are inner feminine power, creativity, focus, and clarity. Inner feminine power provides the foundation for the other three aspects.

Inner Feminine Power

What is power? It is not greed, domination, or control. Power is an energy, an awareness and mastery of self that a person can develop internally. Internal power can then be stretched outward to transform the world. *Power is the knowledge that you*

97

are able to act. Every subsequent act is more powerful than the previous one. Power is the ability to get things done. Magic occurs when you have inner power, and you put energy behind it to create change.

Change for ourselves and for the planet is our challenge and our primary objective as women as the new millennium approaches. To make a shift in our culture, to balance male and female energy for a safer and saner and healthier workplace and world, women need to acknowledge and start using our own strengths. We need to bring our inner power and values out into corporations and the culture at large.

Men are trained from early childhood how to develop, have, and exercise power. As boys, they are raised with the belief that they are entitled to power. Girls are trained to support the gender-biased belief that boys deserve power. Girls are further taught how to develop males' power by giving their own power away, by building the male ego at the expense of their own self-worth and self-esteem. Subsequently, we unconsciously encode these silly, demeaning gender role behaviors into our own children, even in their infancy, beginning with the gender-biased color scheme of pink and blue; interestingly, color systems linking various hues to emotional states claim that pink pacifies people, while blue strengthens them.

Our educational system further supports the gender role stereotypes. Studies have found that teachers pay more attention to boys in class due to their more assertive behavior, and they reward girls for their quiet dependency. Girls are often discouraged from careers in math and science, careers that carry power and financial rewards in our culture.[1]

Due to these cultural and educational biases, by the time a woman reaches adulthood, she shies away from her own power; she feels power is a masculine characteristic and antithetical to being feminine. Power becomes a "dirty word" for most women. Therefore, women try to give our power away and all too often find ourselves waiting to be rescued. Some women want someone else to be responsible for them. Yet, as we give our power away, we also give our energy away. This is called "dependency" and is listed in the psychiatric manual for diagnosis, the *Diagnostic and Statistical Manual of Mental Disorders,* as a personality disorder,[2] even though it could more properly be considered a socialized cultural disorder!

Although women have made progress in many areas, we are still in conflict about acknowledging and exercising our own female strength and power, particularly with men in the workplace. Do you have the "Sleeping Beauty Syndrome"? The symptoms are hard work, loyalty, noncomplaining, and nonuse of power. As Gail Zellman points out in *Women and Sex Roles, Politics and Power:* "Both males and females tend to regard the direct exercise of power as masculine. Women are socialized to strive for and achieve their goals through much more indirect means."[3]

Even in the late 1990s, it is still considered gender inappropriate in our culture for females to be "too" aggressive or "too" assertive. Yet without these attributes, it is difficult to get our needs met or to equal the power males show in the business world in order to get ahead. While aggressiveness is rewarded in male behavior, a woman is demeaned and punished when she uses aggressive behavior. This is equivalent to having a handicap, albeit one imposed by the culture.

"In any situation where someone has power over us, adaptation, survival, or success depends upon meeting their expectations, avoiding angering them, doing whatever is required to get into or stay in their 'good graces,'" explains Jean Shinoda Bolen.[4]

Differences in the Use of Power by Women and Men

Men are usually ascribed with power, which means our society automatically gives them more value and power at birth. Women, on the other hand, have to earn or achieve power in our society. According to research, once power is achieved, men and women deal with it differently. The women who were researched used their power to make other people's lives better.[5]

Because women have been trained and socialized to be "other-directed," we carry that energy with us into power. Where we won't stand up for ourselves, we often will stand up for, or protect, others—whether children, animals, or the Earth as a whole. Women have been the volunteers in this country who have salvaged and saved the victims again and again from the ravages of our patriarchal culture as we have ministered to the homeless, the children, the animals.

We women have the energy of power within us instinctually. We make the choice whether to use it or to become caged. Power gives us the ability to act from our center, not just react to life around us. Power is in the eye of the eagle, not the fear of the mouse.

Inner Lessons

For thousands of years, women have had responsibility without power—while men have had power without responsibility.

ROBIN MORGAN, *A Woman's Creed*

Inner power and autonomy are the results of our own achievement. Fear of success is a fear of risking our own power. A woman's power and freedom increase as her ability to support herself financially increases.

Power is the major factor separating dominant and subordinate groups. Those who dominate demonstrate and acknowledge their power. Subordinates need to hide their power so as not to threaten dominants. Therefore, they learn covert methods of control and attraction. Feminist psychologist Dr. Jean Baker-Miller wrote, "Dominant groups tend to characterize even subordinates' initial small resistance to dominant control as demands for an excessive amount of power!"[6] Therefore, when first exercising or practicing our inner power, we women often feel unsafe or threatened. We fear a loss of male approval.

For women to begin to acknowledge and assume our own inner feminine power, there are four basic lessons for us to learn.

Lesson #1: Mastery of Self/Self-Direction

The first lesson involves choosing between inner power and the approval of others, particularly male approval. You can't have inner feminine power if you are asking others if it is okay. Approval from others is an elusive thing. You must constantly change yourself to fit everyone else's needs. In addition, always trying to please others causes a generalized anxiety about ourselves and our self-esteem, because we are basing our level of self-esteem outside ourselves.

Not only is outside approval elusive, it is also an illusion, since searching for approval is our attempt to fit into another person's belief system. "Approval" relationships, therefore, really serve the other person's needs, since the approval we receive is only given to sculpt or mold our own behavior. When you seek approval from outside yourself—whether for mental recognition, emotional approval, security, spiritual acceptance, or acceptance of your sexual identity—you will get caught in the trap of "never being good enough." We expend a huge amount of energy trying to get fulfilled from approval outside ourselves. Instead, teach yourself inner emotional balance and get your approval from within. Positive affirmations, statements that affirm our intrinsic worth, help us to increase our power. Put yours on a cassette tape and listen to them every morning, or write them on a piece of paper and tape it to your mirror.

It's time for us to *learn to risk,* to take our own actions without the need for approval of others. In so doing, our inner feminine power will begin to flow. We are called upon to take the risk to be all of who we are. But beyond that, when we risk allowing the feminine power to surface again, we bring feminine energy back into balance with masculine energies, which gives us the leverage to save the planet from out-of-control, unbalanced energy.

To experience our inner power, we can jump into our memories of the Amazon Goddess within ourselves. Through this aspect of ourselves—the Amazon Goddess—we have the power to bring our dreams into reality! We are then able to take action in the world with courage and without the constant need for approval.

Lesson #2: Emotions Versus Power

You cannot be living out of your inner little girl and have true inner power. Your inner child needs to be honored, for she holds your spontaneity and your joyous essence, but she is always seeking approval and lives from her emotions, not from power.

You cannot reside in both emotions and power at the same time. *Emotions are our feelings combined with memories of past experiences, which create a response in the present.* I am not saying that emotions are bad, but there are appropriate as well as inappropriate times to feel and work with emotions. If you are in an upset emotional state, you are feeling the *effect* of another person or experience. For example, a woman with inner power knows intuitively that timing is important in projecting her different aspects, and that her little girl does not belong at the boardroom table. Whatever aspect of herself she projects will determine how she is responded to, and staying awake to this awareness can change our lives.

By practicing the exercise from Chapter 3 on awakening your womb power, you can further develop your ability to shift from your emotions into your true inner power.

Lesson #3: Natural Female Aggression/Assertion

As women, we are afraid of acknowledging our own power because we fear men's reaction to it. We fear their anger if they are threatened by our power, or we fear they will abandon seeing us as attractive, sexual women. We are afraid of being labeled a "feminazi."

Men can be terrified of women's power, because they fear that a woman expressing her power will take their male power away from them. Men can always feel strong if women are weak, but if women refuse to act weak, we are accused of emasculating them, of being a "castrating bitch," signifying their strong disapproval and attempt at censure.

A woman expressing her power by being as assertive as a man is derogatorily called a "bitch." But in Mother Nature, a bitch is simply a four-pawed, pad-footed animal who is at her highest state of power in the feminine, such as a lion, cougar, coyote, or wolf. All her senses are in tune with her environment. She is a superior hunter. She is in her warrior state, and, if attacked, she will fight six times as hard as any male. She has within her the real power of the feminine, of Mother Nature, which we women of the human species also have. "Bitch. It's not a negative connotation to anybody who lives in harmony with nature," says Thunder Strikes, a teacher in the shamanic tradition. "How did it get so twisted around? That is the mind game of domination. Those seeking power take a positive powerful attribute and turn it against those they wish to subordinate because of their fear of it. Thus, for the last two millennia, women have been punished the most for their natural, inner feminine power, particularly around sexuality."[7]

When a woman is called a bitch, more likely than not, she is being aggressive. *Aggressive* is defined as "marked by bold determination and readiness for conflict." This echoes the definition of *courage,* "a quality of mind or temperament that enables one to stand fast in the face of opposition."[8] So the next time you have to take a step forward for yourself or your career, define your act in terms of *courage*. When you depress an energy, you become blocked. When you become blocked, you are ineffective and become psychologically depressed. Every psychotherapist knows the cure for depression is to generate activity, to get the energy moving forward in a positive, powerful way. Don't shy away from your own inner power, because it is *the* energy generated to help you take charge of your own life and to achieve your goals. Activate your energy!

Aligning With a Power Animal

This is a simple exercise to help you realign your inner power with the power of the feminine, through alignment with an animal. You can practice the following visualization as a meditation. You can also utilize this technique without doing the research steps #1 and #2. However, if you are willing to invest the time and effort to do those steps first, you will find your visualizations much more powerful and effective when you call on them in real life situations.

1. Choose a female animal that attracts you or that you feel an affinity with. A reminder: All animals are animals of power in that they each have attributes that are unique and special. All animals teach us valuable lessons about ourselves and our own power, especially how to live in balance and proper alignment.

2. The next step, whether you choose a tiger or a turtle, is to learn as much as you can about that animal, par-

ticularly the female of the species. Visit your local zoo, read about it, view videos about it, find pictures. Read books from the shamanic earth traditions that describe the "gifts" or "medicine" of that animal (Sun Bear's *Earth Astrology,* for example). What can this animal teach you? Become familiar with the attributes you want to incorporate into yourself. You may find several animals that you wish to pull into your circle of resources.

3. As a meditation or a "quickie" rebalancing of your energy, close your eyes, breathe deeply several times, and begin to visualize the animal and its strong characteristics. In nature, females are not subservient to males. See the animal's strength when challenged, her physical prowess, her cunning, her instinct, the qualities that make her uniquely what she is.

4. Visualize yourself taking on these positive and powerful traits. If you are visualizing one of the big cats, actually let your body move as she moves. Stretch like a cat, for example. Growl her growl; roar her roar. If you are visualizing a doe deer, let your body assume her stance, head held high, alert and listening for danger. If you are visualizing a beaver, you may want to focus on her gathering and storing food for the winter, her industriousness, and her focus on "getting the job done." Feel that energy in your body. Hold your energy space and relax into it.

5. These are all acts of power and when we emulate them, we build confidence in ourselves and appreciate more what is unique and special about us. Make the visualization as clear and as real as possible so that when you are experiencing fear, anxiety, uncertainty, or confusion, you can employ these traits. This exercise will help you develop power and potential you already have within you. The animal is an ally for you in the sense that it can help you develop those traits and make them come alive in you!

I often align myself with the female lion. Her sleek strength and physical and mental agility inspire me. She can run as fast as a deer, and she is the hunter who returns with dinner for the pride. She is intelligent, powerful, and aggressive. The lion is an old symbol of the goddess, the matriarchy, and feminine power. In matriarchal myths, the Goddess drove a chariot pulled by lions, or she rode naked on the back of her lion.

Patriarchal consciousness has separated women from our wild, feminine nature. Men have placed negative labels on it, and overdomesticated and depressed women's true feminine power. Men have done this out of fear. Now it is time for us to realign the strengths of our female nature, including assertion and natural aggression, and thereby reconnect with ourselves and our natural power. And the next time someone calls you a bitch, take it as a compliment and remember this acronym: BITCH: Being in Total Control of Herself! The lion!

Lesson #4: Learn How to Communicate Power

If you broke down by percentages the average first impressions or observations of one person by another, 7 percent would be based on verbal skills, 33 percent on sound, tone, and manner of speech, and 55 percent on nonverbal communication.[9]

An important observation of the differences between the sexes is the variation in the use of verbal and nonverbal communication and physical distance in men's and women's interactions with others. Men tend to use a hierarchical style of communication, competing or struggling to be one up. Men generally talk more than women, but they use the communication style of reporting or teaching rather than rapport building.[10] In addition. men use more distance and less physical contact in interactions with others, which makes them seem less approachable and less vulnerable. The physical distance they maintain gives them the appearance of aloofness that is needed to hold dominant male power.

Within men's own personal space, men appear to make themselves larger with body postures, while women have been taught to make themselves smaller. For example, we cross our legs, fold our hands together, lower our gaze, or even slouch. These verbal and nonverbal behaviors appear to give men the upper hand with dominant power. But they actually undercut their effectiveness in personal relationships through their failure to establish rapport and, most of all, intimacy.

On the other hand, women generally tend to use verbal communication to build rapport, to connect, to support, and to build relationships.[11] We disclose more information about our lives and ourselves, which helps us connect faster but also makes us seem more vulnerable in men's eyes by revealing more of ourselves.

We also follow this style with nonverbal behavior. Women are more likely to be comfortable with greater physical contact and closer personal distance with others. Research has shown we express more positive feelings about social interactions. In addition, women are generally better able to read and intuit more complex nonverbal behavior from others. However, most subordinate groups are better able to read nonverbal behavior of the dominant group. This is necessary for their own survival.[12]

It only appears that men have more authority because they make themselves less vulnerable and more distant. As men create distance and separateness with their verbal and nonverbal communication, women try to connect, which makes some men retreat further. Women then try harder to connect. This makes us look vulnerable and needy. We lose our power, because we have thrown ourselves out of our energy center in trying to reach and please the other person.

If women are to hold power, we need to change the stereotypical forms of our subservient communication behaviors. There is a simple test for this. When you feel your energy concentrated outside of yourself on another, zap it back to your power center like a boomerang. Use the centering techniques discussed in Chapter 3 and wait quietly, giving the other person time to reach out to you. Also, watch and learn how men use distance and space. When they are distancing themselves, back up, create a vacuum, give them time, and they will come forward if you stop chasing them to connect. Become more mysterious with directness when the time is appropriate. Magnetize.

Hold your own energy space. Don't ask for permission or approval; there is no need to prove anything to anyone. Build on your own centered energy; don't spill it all over in self-pity or victimization. Your attitude and approach to yourself and to life will either drain you or give you inner strength and authority.

As you practice the four lessons just presented, you will grow in your ability to live out of your inner feminine power. This will provide the energy and the basis for claiming your power in the workplace. Now, we will build on the foundation of inner feminine power that you have just explored.

Creativity

There is a vitality, a life force, an energy, a quickening that is translated through you into action, and because there is only one of you in all of time, this expression is unique. And, if you block it, it will never exist through any other medium and be lost. The world will not have it.

MARTHA GRAHAM

Inner feminine power provides the foundation for the other three aspects that women need to cultivate to claim their power in the workplace—creativity, focus, and clarity. Creativity is truly the wellspring of inner feminine power. The symbol of the power of feminine creativity, expressed by the Earth and Mother Nature, explodes around you every day. In creativity resides the energy of life and expression. Creativity wakes us up as souls to our own being and aliveness. You cannot be numb and immersed in the creative process at the same time.

Creativity springs forth from free individuals. In past decades, women were steered towards creating and birthing physical children as our only outlet for creation. While giving birth is an extraordinary creative act, there are other ways for female creative power to birth itself, ways we are only now becoming free enough to manifest in large numbers.

As women, we have huge, *untapped* reservoirs of creativity that many of us have not yet accessed. Although the world around us originates from creativity, from the paintings on our walls to the toasters in our kitchens, women's immense creative genius has been guided down a narrow tunnel, where we have only been rewarded for certain minimal creative accomplishments. The fewer rewards offered to a group for their creativity, the less motivation there is to follow through with creation. The more limitations placed on a group, the more they overadapt to cultural regulations and roles. Therefore, the narrower the role they are allowed, the harder it is for the group to generate their own creativity. This has been women's dilemma until fairly recently. Yes, we were allowed to express ourselves in fashion and makeup (one of the reasons so many women love to shop) and in the arts of homemaking and decorating. But three-quarters of the world of creativity, such as music, art, business, and invention, was shut off to us until fairly recently. In these fields, women went unrecognized, like a river blocked up by a dam. There were no female Mozarts, Picassos, or Hemingways because if you were creative and female, by and large you were not recognized. *Leaders know that the expression of artistic culture influences the direction of the people through their subconscious.* In totalitarian societies, from Nazi Germany to the Soviet Union, artistic culture was tightly controlled for precisely this reason. In America, for most of its history, women were not truly validated for any valued expression, including creativity.

Today we need to recapture our own creativity and move it into our workplace and our professions. To begin with, we need to move out of the mundane and repetitious jobs offered to women that dull our energies—the so-called pink-collar jobs. We come home from these jobs irritable, cranky, and fatigued. The life has been drained out of us and, like robots, we get up the next morning and start over again.

To prevent our creative expression, women have been told over and over that we aren't logical and that our magical creative mind of knowing and intuition is not valuable. And while women have played the role of muse to many famous male artists and businessmen, our genius has lain dormant in our creative capabilities of knowing, passion, and intuition. Because we are connectors, we can easily connect to the creative ether that surrounds our planet, sometimes known as the "collective unconscious," where ideas are stored. We can also connect to the place of magic, the other creative current of life. And when "woman magic" is acknowledged and given permission to come forth into the world, we fulfill our birthing around the entire wheel of women's creativity.

We all have creativity and we all know it, but we've been scared to risk expressing it in the wider world. In the past, many of us have planted our seeds of ideas in men and let them take them to fruition, but so often they've been distorted in the process. It is now our time to carry our own creation in a feminine way into the universe. We must risk doing this for the survival of the feminine, the survival of the Earth. We must lead culture with our art, our writings, and our creations.

To get off the beaten track of our mundane jobs, here are four lessons we can learn to help us open to our creative genius.

Lesson #1: The Law of Use

The creative flow is never lost; it is only submerged. When you open and start using your creativity, the flow begins anew, but we must give it space, time and nurturance. The more we use it, the more it will flow. Practice the following exercise to tap into a creative space.

THE LAW OF USE

1. Follow the steps of the Awakening Womb Power exercise in Chapter 3 to relax you and move your focus into the creative space of your womb. If you practice this, you will soon be able to do it very quickly. Be sure to have pen and paper next to you.

2. Don't search for ideas — just be — as you observe your breath flowing in and flowing out. When ordinary thoughts arise about your day and things you should do, just let them flow through. In the yogic traditions, it is said that our mind is like a little monkey, always chattering. When you go below the chatter, pure creativity exists. To reach this well of creativity, just be, centered in your womb. Don't strain or try; just be. This is a relaxed focus. When you let go and allow this process to unfold, you connect to your own creativity.

3. As creative ideas or insights come to you, jot them down. Don't stop to analyze them. Keep your consciousness in your womb and continue to stay open to what comes through. It is in this precious silence that God, the Great Spirit, speaks to us with clarity, and we can then tap into the ideas of the collective unconscious.

4. Practice this exercise for twenty minutes at a time. Your obsessive self may tell you all the mundane things you should be doing—cleaning, telephoning, working, and so forth. Let it all go, and feel the richness in just being you. Let go of your demons—the ones that want you to clean, the ones that don't want you to be alone. All of them are saying, "You should, you ought to, you could have. . . ." They are all beating you into the ground. When you want to get to know another person, you spend time alone with that person. Therefore, to get to know yourself, you must do the same. You can't chase around outside of yourself to find yourself. You go within—alone. Alone equals "all one." Just relax. This is how you get to know yourself and open to your flow of creativity.

5. You can use a variation of this exercise if you want to find creative ways to solve a particular problem or work on a particular project. Before you enter into your meditative space, clearly state your intent: State the problem or project clearly, state what you are searching for, and ask your inner wise woman to help you access your creative wellspring.

Another excellent technique for unblocking your creative flow is called "The Morning Pages," developed by Julia Cameron and described at length in her book *The Artist's Way*.

Lesson #2: Trust and Believe in Your Creative Ideas

The next step or lesson is to *risk* following your creative vision. Then life will open up. If you stay too structured, you will dry up.

This doesn't mean you have to quit your existing job. Instead, what it means is that you have to risk acting on your creative vision *now*, by setting time aside in your schedule to work on your vision (another reason it's so important to share the housework with others!). As your vision starts turning into substance, the time to do it will increase, and eventually the economic rewards will come as well. So stop listening to your excuses about why you can't live out your creative dream, and instead begin telling yourself all the reasons you can! Helen Keller said it poignantly: "Life is either a daring adventure or nothing."

Lesson #3: Being Your Own Magic—
The Power of Individuality

There are five reactions you will encounter when you project your creativity into the world. People will either love it, hate it, like it, dislike it, or be neutral and not care one way or the other.

Think of Picasso's paintings. They elicit these very same five reactions. Some people love them; some hate them; and some experience other reactions in between. Any work of creative power will not be liked or approved of by everyone. And oftentimes, a person's disapproval says more about that person's past experiences and perceptions than it does about either you or your creation. So approval seeking is a waste of energy, because expressing your creativity is about expressing your inner power, not about getting approval.

So begin today. Risk doing. Stop making excuses or seeking approval. Be your own magic!

Lesson #4: The Simple Formula

The following steps will help you realize your creative goals:

1. Focus on your heart's desire. (Get the prerequisite knowledge necessary.)

2. Use mental discipline and intent.

3. Focus your energy (into action).

4. Your focused energy will turn into material substance and form.

Focus

*Focus is composed of sensing, hearing,
and following the direction of the soul-voice.*

CLARISSA PINKOLA ESTES,
Women Who Run With the Wolves

Focus is a matter of where you put your energy to manifest your dream into reality. Focus is especially difficult for women because so many demands are made upon us from the outside world. Therefore, to focus your energy, you must have a strong inner dream, your heart's desire, to maintain your intent and help you set your priorities.

Once again, this means taking control of your own time and making clear decisions about what, when, and where you will do something. It means knowing that you deserve the time to focus your energy on your dream, and knowing that you have the power behind the energy to actualize that dream. It involves using your will.

"Distraction energy" is anything that takes you away from your goal, your sacred dream. For so many women, the distraction energy is men, relationships, emotional trauma dramas, friends' problems, and so forth. Distraction energy must be handled by visualizing your sacred dream, your goal. *To awaken to your purpose in this lifetime requires tremendous acts of strength.* You need to see your goal in front of you clearly, cutting the distractions. Your mind can only hold one thought or one set of thoughts at a time. Your thoughts are the food you feed your spirit that will actualize your reality. Whether you are ruminating about an emotional drama in your mind or some other problem, visualize your dream, and cancel the negative thoughts and distraction by simply saying, "Cancel, cancel." Keep replacing the distraction thought with your focus, no matter how many times you have to do it.

In actualizing your own sacred dream, first ask yourself what you personally believe in and what you want to achieve in this lifetime. Then, before all the negative thoughts of obstacles overwhelm you, tell yourself you have the competence and the power of intent to achieve your dream. Write down the steps you have to take to achieve your dream. Now, take the first step. When you embark upon your purpose, everything is within your reach.

Focus also means setting boundaries on your time and space. It means saying no to other people's demands and valuing your own creative space.

MORNING CEREMONY: SALUTATION TO THE SUN

This simple yet beautiful ceremony, found in the spiritual practice of many native traditions, will help you set your purpose and focus your energy for the day. Perform this ceremony in the morning when you first wake up.

1. Go outside and face the rising Sun. Close your eyes and breathe deeply. Feel the warmth of the Sun's rays. Breathe in the energy of the birth of a beautiful new day.

2. Silently or aloud thank the Sun for its blessings, its life-giving rays of light and warmth, and express gratitude for the day ahead.

3. Stretch your arms out in front of you towards the Sun and form a triangle with your thumbs and forefingers. Position your hands in such a way that the triangle frames the Sun. *(Caution: Do not look directly at the Sun for any length of time, as this will cause serious damage to your eyes. You should do this with your eyes closed.)*

4. Now you want to draw the energy of the Sun into you. Slowly bring the triangle you have formed with your hands straight to your third eye (the space between and slightly above your eyebrows). This is your intuitive eye that can "see what can't be seen." As you do so, inhale as

though you are also sucking that energy into you. Pause there for a moment, and feel the energy of the Sun activate your third eye.

5. Then bring your hands down the front length of your body (still maintaining the shape of the triangle) and slowly bring the triangle to rest over your womb. As you do this, exhale and visualize that exhalation of Sun energy going into and expanding your womb. Again, pause and feel the Sun energizing and activating your "shamanic root of power."

As you go through steps #4 and #5, visualize as clearly and vividly as you can the warmth, the energy, the power, and the vibration of all that energy being drawn into you.

6. Do this at least five times or until you begin to feel a marked energetic difference. Then, with your eyes still closed, state aloud what you would like to accomplish for the day, setting your focus and intent. Visualize yourself doing and accomplishing your intent. Call in any ancestors or spirit guides who are dancing in the light to help you. Ask for the increased energy and focus you need to accomplish your sacred dream.

7. Thank the Divine for this day, and make an offering to the Great Spirit (the Divine/Goddess/God, or whatever language expresses the universal energy for you). Leave a little pure tobacco, blue corn meal (paho), one strand of your hair, or anything that the Earth can absorb back into herself. This is an energy exchange, your personal "give-away," which symbolizes respect, gratitude, and honoring for that which gives you life and sustenance.

8. As you go through the day, bring your awareness back to your intent and refocus on it. You can always do the Awakening the Womb or Holding the One-Point exercises from Chapter 3 if you need help to stay on track. Enlightenment is staying awake to your purpose on a daily basis.

If it is a cloudy day and the sun is obscured, you can still do this ceremony. The Sun is still there, and its presence still warms the day. You are really doing an energy dance with the Sun, and your ceremony will still be powerful and effective.

Clarity

Women need to lift the veil of their denial and see reality with clear vision and insight. We must see the reality of our roles in this culture and our impact on the Earth's environment. Many of the women I see in my therapeutic practice are in pain because they won't see with clarity. They rationalize and make excuses for the men in their lives. They use denial about what is happening to them in the workplace. They are afraid to take their power and fearful of the word *change*. When we lack clarity, we are asleep. And because of our fear of our own power and autonomy, we women have allowed ourselves to be asleep for generations. But it is our power and our autonomy that we must see clearly and grow up into. We must push our edge if we are to be truly alive.

Because we can so easily be manipulated by fear, by labeling something good or bad, we often subordinate our values and opinions to those of an authority figure, even if what that person says is contrary to our own experience. To begin seeing with clarity, we must question authority; we must question beliefs from outside ourselves. Women much more than men stay in denial. If you don't believe this, look around at our past and our present, at the state of affairs of our country, our world, our Earth. Who have we believed? Who have we followed? Who have we given our power to? Have men followed through with women's priorities in educating the children, supporting our values, and taking care of the Earth, our home?

Getting Clear

We need clarity to see things as they really are, so we can put our feminine power behind change for ourselves and for our world. The following steps will help you begin to see with clarity.

1. Stay in touch with reality, and perceive without pre-conceptions. Step outside of your *role* as wife, mother, secretary, manager. Think about what is really going on around you. Ask yourself about it. See, hear, and feel with clarity, with the observing eye of the eagle, not the small vision of the mouse.

2. If you find yourself rationalizing or making excuses for yourself, you are not using your power. *If you are rationalizing or making excuses for another, you are not using your clarity.* What do you know but don't want to admit?

3. See what area you rationalize in most. Where do you feel most asleep? Wake up. Rattle your own cage, and open the door and step out. Make some positive changes. Why does change make you shrink? Our life stagnates and becomes stuck without the flow of change.

4. If you feel threatened or fearful because you aren't following the beliefs of an outside source, do a clarity check, and ask, "Am I being manipulated by fear, anger, blame, guilt, or shame?"

5. Finally, learn to risk. Take the risk to live your own life, awake, aware, and alive!

Risk, risk anything. Care no more for the opinion of others, for those voices. Do the hardest thing on earth for you to do. Act for yourself. Face the truth.

Katherine Mansfield

To recapture the important points of this chapter:

1. Taking our power in the workplace is crucial to positioning ourselves to facilitate change in the world at large.

2. Inner feminine power means looking within for answers rather than turning to others for approval.

3. You can shift from your emotions to your true inner power by using the centering exercise from Chapter 3.

4. Visualize the strong characteristics of a female animal of power, and remember that BITCH means Being in Total Control of Herself.

5. Learn the verbal and nonverbal cues that help you hold your own energy space.

6. Build on the strengths of being self-deserving, self-accepting, and self-tolerant.

7. We can learn to access huge untapped reservoirs of creativity by reowning our intuition.

8. Go beneath your mind and tune in to pure creativity. Keep a pen and paper nearby to jot down your insights.

9. Risk following your creative vision, and don't be deterred by others' reactions.

10. With focus and clarity, go forward with your sacred dream.

11

External Solutions Through Balancing the Workplace

Life, or the quality of life, depends upon purchasing power.

AMINATA TRAORE,
Seeds: An African Perspective

Matriarchal Task Assignments

Now that you have a sense of how to claim your inner feminine power, you are ready to consider taking some additional steps in claiming your power externally in the workplace. Taking these risks may feel scary at first. *Matriarchal task assignment* is a term used by Native American grandmothers for the tasks they give to their apprentices to help them overcome obstacles or fears. We all have obstacles to overcome in the workplace, such as the dominance and discrimination that cause unequal pay, the glass ceiling, and sexual harassment. Our fears include rejection, abandonment, isolation, and losing our job if we create waves. We can't have two emotions going on at the same time. Let's replace our fears with a positive emotion. Let's overcome our obstacles by learning to turn the energy of fear into a challenge, and obstacles into accomplishments. These are our lessons.

The following matriarchal task assignments can help us break out of gender stereotypes, stuck jobs, and the pink-collar ghetto, and allow us to soar through the glass ceiling. This is like breaking out of a small cocoon into the freedom to fly. To be able to birth your inner power, autonomy, and creativity — to awaken your spiritual goddess, the divine within, your warrior — that is magic. And, with that freedom, you will fulfill your own sacred dream as well as the collective dream of balancing the feminine and masculine energies on planet Earth.

Matriarchal Task #1: Creating a Circle of Women

While it may sound overly simplistic, we must first connect with one another as women by valuing and acknowledging one another's power, as well as our own power, across all levels of the company where we work. We need to join with one another to create a group or circle of women. A circle is a symbol of joining together ceremonially with no hierarchy. It is a collecting of the energy within to form a powerful magic. The circle has always been one of the primary feminine signs. This discussion focuses on creating a support group for women in a corporate setting. If you're self-employed or work for a smaller business, you might gather other women from your neighborhood and talk about ways to help one another reach your goals rather than focusing on more corporate issues.

The priority or purpose of the circle of women is to provide a sacred space to meet with women who are working for positive goals for themselves as well as the other women in your company. This will eventually translate into positive energy for your company, which, by the way, will translate into a changed working world for your daughters who come after you.

As a circle of women, network with one another and support one another. Avoid women who have chosen to identify with the aggressor. These are women who tend to prefer being with men and who have adopted negative male values. Identification with the aggressor is a life survival technique in extreme circumstances (remember Patty Hearst back in the 1970s, who after being kidnapped by the Symbionese Liberation Army ended up joining them, toting a gun, and robbing banks?). In our society, some women identify with the male sex because men have more power in our system. These women treat men as if they had more value, and they undervalue women. These women will not be helpful in a matriarchal circle. Their modus operandi is sabotaging other women. So avoid the pitfall of aligning with them. When assembling your circle, find other women who are willing to respect and value women. Remember, with each woman we put in a higher position, two more can follow. Set up a women's ladder. The group can be a source of information, promotion, guidance, and support for one another. Ask yourselves: How does your company treat women? How do they promote women? Do they offer child care?

Another purpose of your circle could be to find out how and what your company is doing to either improve or further destroy the environment. Our vision as women is to bring into public view both those companies who are having a negative impact and those who are having a positive impact as role models. How do they use the Earth's resources? How environmentally aware are they?

The success of such circles of women lies in the fact that most women find it more inspiring to reach for a dream with someone else. We know how to work diligently for others; in fact, we often work harder for others than we do for ourselves. We need to take this attribute and combine it with other women so that together we can work for one another with the goal of reaching our potential and balancing the workplace.

We see women helping one another throughout corporate America. One of my friends who works at a large savings and loan helped three secretaries become real estate appraisers. She was on the management rung of the corporate ladder, and she used her position to pull up three other women by giving them the right information as well as encouragement. Thus, by working together and helping one another, we are able to better support our children and pull one another out of poverty or financial inequality. This is known as a women's success ladder.

Begin visualizing a circle of women in every department of every corporation, in small offices, in government offices, in schools, in retail stores, helping one another, networking, negotiating with management, changing our environments, getting involved together, making a difference for our daughters and setting an example for the world that women can have the inner power to change the world if we stick together!

A suggested format for this positive circle of women would be to meet on the first and third Wednesday of every month. The focus of your circle might be to help your company break through the glass ceiling and dissolve other barriers before the year 2000. These circles are not rap sessions in which all you do is complain and return to work as victims. You can alternate leaders at each gathering to give each woman the feeling and experience of inner power as well as keeping the group from becoming noncircular or hierarchical.

First, get the facts about your company or your circumstances. You might send for your company's prospectus or year-end report, or go to the personnel department and get a list of officers, directors, vice presidents, executives, managers, partners, and so forth. Find out how many women are in the ranks of the top one-third of your company. Is it equal to the percentage of women supporting and working for the company? Or are the workers and support staff overwhelmingly women while the high-paying jobs are filled by men? Take a long, hard look at who you are working for. Their prejudices and beliefs will be mirrored by those they choose for management. Then, use your circle to help them change to a point of balance.

Next, begin negotiating with management and the top officers at your company. Ask for meetings every two months to discuss putting qualified women in upcoming career openings. Negotiate new training programs for support staff and pink-collar women so that all have an avenue for moving up the ladder. Your company will then have an investment in their career and future. Also, negotiate for child care to free you from worry, so you can focus your intent on your success.

To negotiate effectively, it is important to negotiate with clarity, inner power, focus, and creativity, the qualities we explored in Chapter 10. Pressure applied in the right places works much better than hostility. Communicate with the officers and directors of the company by writing letters to them on a regular basis. Let them know what is really going on in the trenches and how attitudes and work could be improved. Don't be afraid. They need to keep in touch with their people for clarity.

Show your company how valuable long-term employees who care about the company can be—employees whose attitude is "I'll work twice as hard for you if you will also work for me." When employers know their employees and both work for the other, the whole environment changes. This is the power of the circle.

Matriarchal Task #2:
Celebrating Women's Equality Day

All women in all professions should take the day off on August 26th, Women's Equality Day. We should all do this every year. Taking this day off provides a gentle but forceful reminder of how many women are in the work force and how necessary and valuable we all are, no matter what position we hold. It provides a reminder of how powerful we can be if we connect and support one another, a reminder to the cold corporation to listen, to communicate. This also reminds our government and our

politicians that we are a majority and we are not afraid to act together. They will take notice of empty seats, slower work, no support staff, no cleanup, and no coffee already made! Do it in fun
and good humor, but do it. Do it for your daughters, for the future, even if you are fearful. We need to balance our workplace.
August 26th is Women's Equality Day! Enjoy it! While the day
hasn't yet received much media coverage, women in other countries have used this method of demonstrating their empowerment.

History has shown that pressure by women on our federal
government, politicians, and the courts has made it impossible
for the business community to ignore women. Sometimes we
have to change our culture from the top down. At one time we
had to change the laws of our country to eliminate master-slave
relationships. Today we have to change our society to eliminate
dominant-subordinate relationships.

Matriarchal Task #3: Take "Response-Ability"

If we feel we have been discriminated against in the past or
are currently being discriminated against, we must take legal action against the company. In order to do this, keep a clear record
of all prejudicial actions. Write the day, time, and person you
spoke with. If a male is promoted over you, question the promotion, evaluate it, wake up, and stay aware. As I've stated earlier, most women don't even realize they are being discriminated
against until we open our eyes and see with clarity.

This includes sexual harassment. We must take legal action
to make our workplace safe. Contact your circle of women or a
women's organization for help. (See Resources in the Appendix
at the back of the book.) Take action. Don't be a wimp! You and
I face these problems today because many women before us were
passive. The choices and freedoms we have today are due to
those courageous women who did take action, who faced their
fears, and who did it for us.

When women are passive about their environment, the energy stays the same for the next generation of women, and for the next generation of young girls after that. When women of the past have pushed hard enough to change the laws, and women of the present have worked to enact new laws to benefit us, it is our responsibility to see to it that these laws are followed by the companies or businesses we work for. If we as women do not support these laws, the whole energy behind the change is lost. It takes the courage of all women to change things.

Thus, say to yourself every day, "I transform the energies of my fears into my own strengths. I will hold my space and challenge discrimination now with courage. This is my own way of gaining energy and power." Remember, power equals the ability to act. By acting, we take responsibility for our lives, our workplace, and the balancing of masculine and feminine energies.

Matriarchal Task #4:
Choosing and Changing Our Profile as Women

As women, we need to evaluate our career goals. If we are going to be working, as statistics say we will be, until retirement, we might as well move ahead in our job or follow our sacred dream. The following lessons are vital steps to take in achieving the most we can in our careers.

Lesson #1: Have an action plan for your career. Develop intention. Where do you want to be in one year, in two years, in five years, in ten years? How are you going to get there? Do you need to go back to school or get more training? *Direction* increases your sense of being alive and seizing your dreams. Write down your dreams and then map the path for getting to them.

Lesson #2: When deciding upon a career, an important factor to consider is where money is controlled in a company. If you have authority over a financial aspect and can show financial results, you are on a faster growth track in comparison to the personnel department or public relations, which are more stereo-typically female jobs. One study done by the Department of Education revealed that women who took more than eight college credits of math earned more money.[1]

When evaluating a job within an organization or company, look at it in terms of the amount of movement potential it provides. Does the job carry possibilities for *future* reward and growth?

It is also important to remember that typically male professions tend to pay more than typically female professions. But the most important question you can ask yourself is, what would you do if money weren't the issue? What is your passion, and how can you make money from it?

Lesson #3: Wake up to gender stereotyping by becoming more active in your work and less reactive. Risk taking your power. And be careful not to fall into stereotypical sex roles.

Act competent and be achievement-oriented. Always learn the job above yours, as well as your own. Instead of complaining about a manager, align with her. Ask her about her job, about how she handles political problems and employees. Think of yourself as a candidate for that position when she is promoted. Know and be aware of what is happening in upper management and make yourself known to them.

When a project is offered, always pick the project with the highest priority to the company. Be a problem solver. Don't get put in a manual or technical skill job. Chances are, as a woman, you might get stuck there. Remember, the definition of *passive* is "not characterized by or engaged in normal activity." One thing you can count on, if you are passive, you will be passed by for that next promotion.

Ask yourself what kind of impact you are making in your work environment. Your impact reflects your creativity, your ability to achieve and change your own circumstances. What changes can you make to increase your positive impact both within yourself and in your external presentation of your work?

Lesson #4: Learn to negotiate. There are many books, tapes, and seminars on the art of negotiation. One of the clearest diagrams of negotiation structure I found is in the book *Women and the Art of Negotiating.*[2] Look it over. The next time you want to negotiate something such as a pay raise, write it out, using the map and instructions provided in the book.

Put Your Money Where the Women Are

For those women who invest in businesses or companies through stocks or mutual funds, invest your money only in companies with practices and policies that support women employees, provide strong career support, and promote women to executive positions while utilizing the Earth's resources responsibly ("Green" companies).

There are a number of mutual funds that look for just these qualities in the array of companies on the stock market. (See the Resources listed in the Appendix for ideas on where to start.)

Women's Economic Power: The Best Kept Secret

There is one major arena where women have a great deal of potential power. This is in the arena of their consumer choices. Women are the major shoppers and purchasers of products and goods in our country. American women's purchasing power is greater than the gross domestic products output of any other country. We have the power as women to make or break the success of corporations. We also have the influence to put pressure on states and other countries to honor women's issues.

Buy products and services from those companies that are "female friendly." Boycott companies that have a glass ceiling for

women employees. Check to see about the large and small companies you buy from. Where you put your money is where you
put your energy. Use it wisely to support the values of equality
and advancement for women.

Do you realize that we buy millions of dollars worth of products from companies who do not have women as executives or as
members on their boards of directors. In grocery stores, we choose
among hundreds of products that are produced by only a handful of companies. For example, the Nestle company is rated as
one of the worst companies for women's advancement in the important book *The Feminist Dollar* by Phyllis and Margaret Katz.
The Nestle company makes such products as chocolate, Baby
Ruth and Butterfinger candy bars, Libby's canned goods, Stouf-
fer's Lean Cuisine, Contadina products, Alcon Opti-free contact
solution, Alpo, Mighty Dog Food, and many other products.

Unilever is another example of a company that had no
women on its board of directors as of 1997 and low ratings in
The Feminist Dollar. They are not supporting women, so why
should we support them? They produce Mrs. Butterworth's
syrup products, Country Crock, Promise, Breyer's, Good Humor
ice creams, Birds Eye products, Lipton products, and Lawry's
products.

As of 1997, Proctor & Gamble had only two women on its
board of directors and no women among its top-paid executives.
Another strike against them is their refusal to stop animal testing. Animals are harmed to create their products. Other companies with similar products do not use animal testing. Proctor &
Gamble products include Duncan Hines baking products, Crisco,
Pringles chips, Maxwell House, Sanka, and Yuban, along with
Ivory, Safeguard, Noxzema, Oil of Olay, Clearasil, Max Factor
and Cover Girl make-ups, Crest and Gleam toothpastes, and
Vicks cold products. Pepto-bismal, Metamuscil, and Aleve pain
killer are also made by Proctor & Gamble.

These are but a few examples, so you can imagine the tremendous size and power of these major corporations. By buying their products, you are supporting their unbalanced structure and the belief that women are not worthy to share in the executive echelons of their companies, as well as giving your approval for their destructive environmental policies.

Nationally and internationally, we can decide which states and countries we want to give our money to. Would you tell me why any woman would want to buy products from China, which our government has prominently put in the position of favored trading status, when they allow the killing of baby girls and have one of the worst human rights records for women? Why would we want to buy products from Thailand when one of their major industries is the sex tourist industry using young teenage girls. Don't spend your hard-earned tourist dollars in countries where your sisters don't have an equal chance. Protest with your dollars!

Women have tremendous strength because while men head the companies that make most of the products, we buy them. Why not use that leverage to change the world for your children? Buy products from companies that truly respect women and that respect our environment. As Phyllis Katz puts it in *The Feminist Dollar*, "The message is that companies that want our hard-earned dollars will have to take some steps to show that they care about and respect women—enough to trust them with all job descriptions."[3]

Alternative Solutions to Women's Work: Starting Your Own Business

There is a fascinating, true story about the women of the Afikpo Ibo tribe in Nigeria, which explains a great deal about women, dependence, business, and control. The Afikpo Ibo tribeswomen made pottery and traded it. They also farmed for the family. In their society, yams were used for ritual and were considered a prestigious crop that was much in demand. The men, therefore, cultivated the yams and controlled the income from them.

When the women traded their pottery, they began traveling farther, which put them in contact with outsiders, who encouraged them to cultivate the cassava plant, the source of tapioca. The men looked down on this work and said the women could keep the profits. The crop brought the women and their children much financial success and consequently independence. Since then, the husbands have found it very difficult to keep their wives in their formerly subordinate status in the home.

The women produced a crop that was of great value to the outside world. And because they controlled the product, the money they made was their own profit to keep. This financial gain equaled freedom and independence from their previously subordinate positions, for themselves and their children.[4] This story teaches us that some women would take their inner power and be less subservient if they had access to better economic opportunities. It tells us that we don't all *choose* subordinate positions, but that they have been a part of women's role and have distanced us from the world of money and power. The greater ability women have to be self-supporting, the more our influence increases.

The tribal story also reveals that products for use and exchange outside the home carry more value than products or services used within the home.[5] To have financial power, we must produce goods or services that have high market value, and we must control what we produce and the ensuing monetary profits.

Today, over five million women in the United States have followed this formula and started their own businesses. Their companies are now generating more employment than the Fortune 500 companies.[6] Businesses owned by women employed 15.5

million workers in 1994 and generated nearly 1.4 trillion dollars in sales. According to Janet Harris Lange, president of the National Association of Women Business Owners, women are more likely to succeed in their own businesses because they will admit when they need help.[7] Many of these women entrepreneurs had a skill they had developed in the home, or a skill they were not being paid equally for in the workplace, so they ventured into the outside world on their own. This is an option for all women.

Think of your own skills, and write them down. Which skills would be in most demand in the outside world? How could you begin, even on a small scale, to test your market. Go to the library, buy some books on starting your own business, or take a Small Business class at your local college.

Just take one step at a time, and don't let your inner demons tell you that you can't do it. Visualize your business and only think in positive terms. Don't share your plans with others unless you can count on their support, because many people will tell you why you can't be successful on your own, sometimes even out of good intent.

Remember, Mrs. Fields started making cookies in her own kitchen! Each one of us has some skill that could be turned into a business.

Remember to think of ecologically progressive ideas. This is not only to your profit and benefit, but to your great-grandchildren's benefit. (Who in Washington, D.C., or in major corporate boardrooms thinks that far ahead?)

Heaven on Earth Restaurant

Let me tell you about one woman's success story. Her name is Christine Jackson, and fourteen years ago, she bought a run-down restaurant building on Interstate 5 in Oregon. The restaurant had already failed eight times. She worked hard, developed a sophisticated country atmosphere, put holiday lights out all year round so her building was noticeable, and served the best homemade specialties twenty-four hours a day. Her restaurant became famous for the biggest cinnamon rolls in Oregon, which she makes in the dining room so customers can watch and smell, and for her apple butter.

Christine then branched out with her apple butter to other stores and restaurants, which she markets under the name Apple Butter Farms. To attract more of the tourists driving on Interstate 5, she built an old frontier town and shops around her restaurant, along with a picnic area, barbecue, and petting zoo.

After being so successful herself, she wanted to teach others how to establish or expand their own restaurants, so she started her own consulting service, called Diversified Restaurant Services. Her secret to success was "giving up the image of being important and helping others learn to develop their potential." That statement captures the essence of feminine power and women's management techniques!

Guess how I met her? I was at a restaurant in Los Angeles with my husband and another couple when she came over to our table to give us a jar of her apple butter along with a flyer on her restaurant and services. What Christine did was to buck gender roles and stereotypes and to extend her physical space and energy outward. To act, not react. To think independently, not be dependent upon.

Stretch your imagination to its farthest limits with what you would like to be doing and, today, make one step in that direction. Take an action beyond just thinking or fantasizing, whether it be making a phone call or doing some research. Tomorrow, take one more action. Move the energy towards your goals. This will fulfill your sense of self, as an accomplishment each day or each week increases your self-esteem. Going in a forward direction increases your sense of being alive! Keep pushing your edge!

To recapture the important points of this chapter:

1. It's time to take risks. "Matriarchal task assignments" can help you overcome your fears and any obstacles society places in your path.

2. Connecting with other women by creating a circle of women gives us the added power of solidarity in the workplace. We can help one another make advances that will serve us all.

3. Celebrate Women's Equality Day on August 26th.

4. Take action when your rights at the workplace are violated. Do this for yourself and for your sisters, daughters, and all women to come.

5. Consider your career goals in light of your life as a whole. Which job carries the best possibilities for future reward and growth, both financial and personal?

6. Invest in women. Help set in motion a cycle where we women raise one another up.

7. Consider whether you'd like to start your own business. Stretch your imagination, and take the first steps.

PART FOUR

Our Place in Our World

About Part Four

In the first three parts of this book, we have explored several major dimensions of your life as a woman. Now it is time to look at how we can participate as women in the larger world. Due to time constraints, as women we tend to view our lives within the framework of our relationships, families, homes, and communities, while sometimes ignoring the larger perspective of the world's influence upon our lives. Yet the outside world affects us deeply and personally. Decisions made at the top levels of local, state, and federal governments filter down to affect our daily lives in the most personal of ways. War takes our husbands and our children away, sometimes forever. Military spending increases our individual tax burden, cutting into our personal income for our family's necessities and also making it mandatory that many of us work to provide two incomes for our family. Governmental laws concerning abortion and birth control determine our access to career opportunities in the workplace as well as the degree of independence we can exercise. Social security policy decisions affect the elderly and determine whether our older parents will be able to afford to live independently or will be dependent on care in our home. As women, therefore, it is crucial that we understand the world in which we live.

Unfortunately, some women are essentially asleep, unaware of how our society is structured, nationally and globally. Many of us accept without question the organizational structures of power in the larger world. By this point, you have read the first three parts of this book and learned the importance of empowering yourself in your personal life, in your family, and in the workplace. Now it's time to wake up to how governmental and cultural structures operate and how they personally affect each and every one of us. The feminist movement has brought many of these issues to our attention. As we approach the next millennium, it is up to all of us to connect with women worldwide to assess where we stand politically, legally, and economically. Then we can begin to take action. In the final chapters of this book, you will learn what you can do to play a crucial and significant role in creating change so that our children and the many species that share this planet with us can continue to survive on our beloved Mother Earth.

12

Awakening to Our Lives in the United States

*From a historical perspective, despite the obstacles,
subordinate groups have tended to move towards greater
freedom of expression and action, although this progress
varies greatly from one circumstance to another. There were
always some slaves who revolted; there were some women
who sought greater development or self-determination.
Most records of these actions are not preserved by the
dominant culture, making it difficult for the subordinate
group to find a supporting tradition and history.*

DR. JEAN BAKER-MILLER

A Look at Our History in America

For women born in the United States, practices against women such as clitoridectomies and female infanticide might sound barbaric. Yet we quickly forget how far we, as American women, have journeyed since the birth of our nation.

In fact, the founding mothers of the United States of America were considered "legal chattels," which means property of their husbands. No Pilgrim women were allowed to sign the Mayflower Compact. We were not allowed to work without our husbands' permission, and when we did, our wages belonged to them. Only men could divorce women; we could not begin divorce proceedings ourselves. We were not allowed an education; only men were educated. We were not allowed to vote in any federal elections in the United States until 1920, and by 1996 women had voted in only 19 of this country's 42 presidential elections. It took women seventy years of fighting nineteen all-male Congresses to win the right to vote. Our right to vote is indeed precious, and we owe it to our foremothers to exercise it at every election.

In the 1800s and as late as the 1930s, one of the many issues of freedom facing our grandmothers was birth control. State laws prohibited the distribution of birth control information, even by doctors, and prohibited the sale of contraceptive devices. It wasn't until 1937, with the help of Margaret Sanger, founder of Planned Parenthood, and Katharine Houghton Hepburn, mother of actress Katherine Hepburn, that U.S. legislators voted to end the federal ban.[1]

Considering our past, we should be able to empathize with and relate to women around the world who still live in positions of powerlessness and fear. Our mothers, grandmothers, and great-grandmothers were once in their place, and if it were not for the work of many women before us, *we might still be there too.*

Consider the flavor of this letter that Abigail Smith Adams, wife of President John Adams, wrote to her husband in 1776 as the Second Continental Congress was debating the Declaration of Independence: "I long to hear that you have declared an independency, and by the way, in the new code of laws which I suppose it will be necessary for you to make, I desire you would remember the ladies and be more generous and favorable to them than your ancestors. Do not put such unlimited power into the hands of husbands. Remember all men would be tyrants if they could. If particular care and attention are not paid to the ladies we are determined to foment a rebellion, and will not hold ourselves bound to obey any laws in which we have no voice or representation."

John Adams's return letter stated: "As to your extraordinary code of laws I cannot but laugh. . . . Depend on it, we know better than to repeal our masculine systems."

Abigail's return letter began: "I cannot say that I think you are very generous to the ladies, for, whilst you are proclaiming peace and good will to men, emancipating all nations, you insist upon retaining an absolute power over wives."[2]

Our Government Today

Are we fully emancipated today? Our United States government was founded on the premise that "taxation without equal representation" was wrong, and yet women retain the distinction of being the most underrepresented major population group in the top echelons of government in the United States as well as the world. In the United States, women account for *over half* the population, yet in our government we are and have historically been totally underrepresented in every aspect of power and decision making. Take, for example, the powerful fact that as of 1997 only 165 women have served in the U.S. House of Representatives since its inception. Compare that to the 10,156 men who have been the lawmakers in Congress since its beginning.[3] In the U.S. Congress, before the 1992 elections, women held only 5 percent of the seats in the House of Representatives. While the 1992 elections doubled that number to 10 percent, and in 1996 the percentage increased to 11.7, as a majority group we are still vastly outnumbered and underrepresented. In 1997, nine women (9 percent) served in the 100-member U.S. Senate. Prior to the 1992 elections, no more than two women had ever served in the U.S. Senate at the same time. On the U.S.

Supreme Court, there are only two women out of nine justices. Although we are making inroads, we still have relatively very little power to influence major decisions in our government. It is a democracy with a male face!

Anne Wilson Schaef, in her renowned women's studies book *Women's Realities,* described our governing system as "The white male system, which controls almost every aspect of our culture. It makes our laws, runs our economy, sets our salaries, and decides when and if we will go to war or remain at home. It decides what is knowledge and how it is to be taught."[4]

Decisions and Economics of War

Now, let us take a look at how women, as followers, have fared under this system and why we ought to have an equal voice in the government's decision-making process as it affects every aspect of a woman and her children's lives. Specifically, let us look at war.

The United States has been involved in nine major wars since the founding of our country. As the millennium approaches, that amounts to one major war every twenty-four years:

1. The Revolutionary War
2. The War of 1812
3. The Civil War
4. The Spanish-American War
5. World War I
6. World War II
7. The Korean War
8. The Vietnam War
9. The Persian Gulf War

Women have not had significant power in the decision-making process of any of these wars, nor have we been allowed any positions of authority in conducting war strategy. The issue of sex discrimination towards women serving in the military has dominated headlines in the late 1990s.[5] But for most of this country's history, women were not allowed in the military, and we have instead provided the support troops in the background. During World War II, for example, women supported the war at home by filling the jobs vacated by our male soldiers when they left to fight. But when the soldiers returned, women were told they were no longer competent enough to keep their jobs. "During the course of each of our American wars, women have been told how important their services are to the winning of the war. Their patriotism, courage, and loyalty are widely praised. The praise, however, is always short-lived. As soon as the hostilities end, so do the compliments and the jobs."[6]

So far during this century, there have been 250 wars fought throughout the world in which an estimated 109,746,000 lives have been lost.[7] Since World War II, some 160 wars have been fought, resulting in over 25 million deaths.[8] To fuel these wars, the United States exported 53 percent of the weapons we produced. In order to *stop* a pending sale of weapons to another country, each House of Congress must vote against it by a two-thirds majority. If Congress takes no action, the sale is considered approved. We need to reconsider this "easy sale" policy and implement guidelines to be used before selling weapons to other countries. With the collapse of the Soviet Union, the U.S. now overwhelmingly dominates the weapons market. Ruth Leger Sivard reported: "The display of weaponry in the Gulf War clinched the U.S. standing in weapons technology. The U.S. is easily Number One in the world arms market. In fact, in 1994 U.S. arms exports were not only the highest of any country but also were well above the total arms exports of *all* 52 other exporting countries combined."[9] A large chunk of the United States economy depends on war and the death of others. As writer Marilyn Waring pointed out: "So death by war has a mathematical value. Other death, by poverty, starvation, thirst, homelessness—is not of the same order. Every minute thirty children die from want of food and inexpensive vaccines. And every minute the world's military budget absorbs [untold millions] of the public treasury. This is war."[10]

On the other side of war is the peace that many political leaders have spoken about for years. But we must not listen to their rhetoric. Instead, we need to watch their actions. After all, it was in the 1920s, just after World War I, that disarmament discussions began between male governments. And they have been talking about it ever since, while at the same time they have been producing and stockpiling weapons. We have had years of an arms race and rapid nuclear escalation. During the 1980s, more military hardware was bought and sold worldwide than food, all while governments talked of peace. In 1983, for example, world military expenditures exceeded $700 billion and were still over $700 billion in 1994.[11] Despite a decline in the first five years of the decade due to the end of the forty-five-year Cold War, world military expenditures in 1995 still amounted to more than $1.4 million per minute. North America (Canada and principally the U.S.) represented almost half of worldwide military spending.[12]

In 1995 the U.S. defense budget was $270 billion, while the budget for environmental protection and toxic waste cleanup was only $7 billion, according to Congressman Anthony Beilenson's report. According to Waring, "The doubling of the United States' national debt, from $914 billion in 1980 to $1.841 trillion in 1985, was due more to the growth in military expenditures than to any other factor."[13] Yet, as has already been pointed out, women have not had the power to make or influence major decisions in the government in the military arena. And if we had?

Women's voting record in the United States shows we are more likely to vote against weapons or military build-up.[14]

Why are the weapons buildup and war such critical issues? Why is the place our government spends the majority of women's tax dollars so important? Because this vast military spending allocates precious resources that could have gone towards solving other problems, and women's voices have not been represented in the setting of these priorities.

There are now enough weapons and bombs to destroy the Earth and ourselves twelve times over. Did you vote for that? Where have our government's priorities been? They certainly haven't been in education, children, family, or ecology programs. On the average, at least 13 million refugees from wars are fleeing from violent conflict; the majority of these refugees are women and children. We can see by where the money is being spent where our government's priorities lie. Our unbalanced male majority government has put power, war games, and weapons of destruction ahead of human life and suffering, ahead of education, children's needs, and, most important, the survival of the planet.

Stephen Hawking, in his audio book *Black Holes and Baby Universes,* speaks about the Doctrine of Diminished Responsibility, Stress, and Aggression. Natural selection has developed a variety of characteristics, such as aggression. Aggression would have given us a survival advantage in cave dweller days, and so would have been favored by natural selection. The tremendous increase in our powers of destruction brought about by modern science and technology, however, has made aggression a very dangerous quality — one that threatens the survival of the whole human race. The trouble is, our aggressive instincts seem to be encoded in our DNA, which changes by biological evolution only on a time scale of hundreds of thousands of years. But our powers of destruction are increasing on an evolution of information time scale, which is measured in decades. Unless we can use our intelligence to control our aggression, the future of the human race looks bleak.[15]

Still, there's hope. The hope is the untapped power of women. Studies show that when women have control of resources and money, the welfare of children and family improve greatly.[16] In addition, women are more oriented towards equal relationships as opposed to vying for dominance or power over another, while men tend to be territorial creatures, creating, marking, and defending their territories. Men tend to be more competitive and to strive for dominance and power among themselves. All these qualities are antithetical to cooperation and to the peace process, while being conducive to power games and military buildup.

Whether these qualities are innate or conditioned has been debated for years within the field of psychology. Perhaps we will not really know for two or more generations, when it is possible to observe the effect of young girls and boys who have been trained to share caretaking responsibilities and when healthier female and male role models have been depicting caregiving behavior. Some will argue that these are oversimplified generalizations, but at this point in our history, they seem worth exploring further.

External Solutions

Tribal stories of the Cherokee and other matriarchal tribes describe what seems to us today to be a very unique way of balancing masculine and feminine energies on their governing councils. The majority of each council was almost always female, for the Cherokees knew that the women, the mothers of the sons who would go to war and the wives of the men who would fight, would only vote for war if war was the only viable option.

Research indicates that we need at least 35 percent women in a governmental body to make any headway in balancing public policy and governmental decisions. As women, we must now assume the responsibility of balancing our decision-making bodies, such as our own government, the Congress, with both masculine and feminine energies. We need to balance each other's characteristics, strong points, and weaknesses in order to create a world more harmonious to all. "Mankind" must evolve into "humankind," and our decisions must now include the other children of the Earth—the plants, the animals, and the environment—all of which suffer from our wars.

How can we achieve this? And how do we begin?

First, women must take their responsibility for voting in each and every election very seriously. Voting is one of the major ways each and every one of us can have an impact on our government. The 17 percent "gender gap" in voting put President Clinton back in office in 1996. The gender gap continues to make a difference between candidates winning and losing elections. Remember, from the year 1848, when Elizabeth Cady Stanton held the first Women's Rights meeting, it took the women of America seventy-two years to get the right to vote, which was finally won in 1920. Women have the power behind their votes to have a great impact on pay equality, their careers, health care, and the environment.

Second, we must move out as women into the larger arena of government, where the power and the decision making are taking place. We can do this by becoming aware of and actively involved in local, state, and federal issues, and then supporting the election of women who carry our values into the legislative positions of power. It is imperative that large numbers of women join with men to add their energy, the energy of the feminine, to balance all governmental decision-making bodies. Don't ignore local politics; if you start to get involved with local issues, you will soon learn just how much impact one person can have.

Within our own communities, women have already become more involved in city councils, as mayors, and on school boards.

In our state legislatures, more women are being elected, and as of 1997 we held 18 percent of the state senate seats and 22.6 percent of the state assembly seats. After a surge in 1992, the number of women holding statewide elected executive office fell slightly,[17] and that decline has continued.

Ask yourself if you might be ready to run for political office. Congresswoman Pat Schroeder of Denver, Colorado, who retired in 1996, never expected to be in the House of Representatives. While raising her family, she became involved in making a difference within her community as a political activist. She then ran for U.S. Congress. Although in her first campaign she did not have the support of the Democratic National Committee, her family and friends helped, and she ultimately was elected to twelve terms in the U.S. House of Representatives. This is only one success story. There are many other stories of other women who wanted to help others and pursued this desire for the greater good of all.

Finally, inspire yourself and other women to take the risk to join together in the affairs of our larger family—the community, the state, the country, the world. We need a new set of values and the power of the feminine to balance our governmental system. For years, men have been talking peace on the one hand while devoting immense resources to weapon proliferation and war on the other hand. It is up to us women to enforce the principles and practice of peace and to put feminine energy behind positive environmental activism.

After all, for years women have quietly cared for the casualties of a male government. We have organized charities and performed volunteer work for these numerous casualties—for children, for the elderly, for the environment. To minimize the casualties of the dominant "only for profits and power" mentality, women now need to change and balance the system from the top down, not the bottom up.

What else can we do?

We can financially support women candidates who advocate and promote our values and opinions. One of the major obstacles to women running for office has been a lack of financial backing and funding. To solve this problem, several women's organizations have been founded to help fund women candidates. For example, EMILY's List (which stands for Early Money Is Like Yeast) is an open membership group of Democratic women who financially support female Democratic candidates. The women's group called The Wish List helps female Republican candidates. The emergence of women into the political arena coincided with the growth of women's groups and organizations which were willing to support and fund their campaigns.

In addition, we can join women's organizations and environmental groups. The higher the member count, the stronger the lobbying power these organizations have in Congress for women's issues and environmental legislation. They educate women on the process of running for political office by giving campaign skills workshops for candidates and volunteer supporters.

Finally, we can keep abreast of local, state, and federal legislation. An organization called 20/20 keeps track of federal legislation and keeps us informed about when and where to call or write to stop destructive legislation or encourage positive initiatives. Buy a dozen blank stamped postcards from the post office, address them to your representatives, and send them to your senator or congressperson when legislation that is important to you comes up for a vote.

It is incumbent upon us that we make our voices heard. Simple, yes. But have most of us done it? No! Now it is our turn to make and influence the decisions! Consider Pearl S. Buck's words from 1938: "To continue to bear children only to have them slaughtered is folly. But to take as a solemn task the preventing of war would be an achievement unmatched. In the process women would become inevitably concerned in human welfare, to the betterment of all society as well as themselves. It is the only hope I can see of the end of war."[18]

Inner Solutions:
Healing Women's Internalized Male Values

One of the main themes running through our culture is that men are important, deserve power and authority, and are of value. The covert theme concerning women, in contrast, is that we are passive and of no value; we are not to be trusted, especially by each other, according to this distortion. Unfortunately, we have weakened our own power by competing with one another for male approval and alliances. Learning to support and trust one another as women is an important step in changing this dynamic.

"Divide and conquer" has worked well on women for centuries, because we have absorbed and internalized imbalanced and dysfunctional belief systems about ourselves and other women. In the past, we have been hesitant to give other women authority or power because of this ingrained conditioning and our beliefs about feminine energy.

Open your heart to push a sister ahead of you. Give your time to support a female candidate. Have the courage inside yourself to call yourself a feminist and support feminine energy in the world. We should not be ashamed of our gender or feel guilty stating that we support one another. Men have supported one another for years with "good ole boy" networks. But the dominant cultures always act to shame subordinates who try to rise to power. Again, consider the example of the word *feminazi*. Putting the word *feminist* together with the word Nazi is a sophisticated mind trick designed to link women who support other women with the terrible atrocities of the Nazi Party. This is an attempt to discourage us from identifying ourselves as feminists. Have enough self-esteem to refuse to buy into this tactic of shaming. Have the inner strength to state your values and beliefs and have the courage to vote and work for them. Freedom requires us to continue to have the courage to take the mantle of power and speak our own truths. It is our responsibility to the women of the future.

To recapture the important points of this chapter:

1. Women have been underrepresented in our government since the founding days of our nation. It's time for a change.

2. War has been supported by the patriarchy. The more women participate, the greater the chances for peace.

3. Consider how to become more involved in your community, as an activist, a candidate, a financial contributor, or a volunteer. Pay attention to local, national, and global issues.

4. It's our turn. It's up to us to vote for a more balanced Congress and government. Never pass up a chance to vote.

5. Take pride in being a feminist and working to support other women.

13

Awakening to the Fate
of Women on the Planet

Women constitute half the world's population,
perform nearly two-thirds of its work hours, receive
one-tenth of the world's income, and own less
than one-hundredth of the world's property.

UNITED NATIONS REPORT,
Program of Action for the Second Half
of the UN Decade for Women

There are over 2.5 billion women in the world, and in many countries we are still considered to be property of the male, whether father, husband, or brother. With inhumane discrimination and inferior status for women prevailing around the planet, women's second place role in family, social, political, and economic spheres is universal. A recent United Nations Development Report states that there is no country that treats women as well as it treats men.[1]

In India, women's status remains extremely low, and women are still thought of primarily as commodities. In fact, there is growing concern about the common practice of dowry deaths, where a bridegroom kills his bride if her family cannot provide enough material possessions, such as TV sets, VCRs, or money.

He is then free to remarry and collect another dowry.[2] An article in the *New York Times* reported, "According to Indian human rights groups, 5,000 women are killed every year in disputes over dowries, mostly by men, but only a handful of cases ever result in conviction."[3] Indian widows, who are often young women or children, have twice the death rate of married women. Violence against widows is alarming. They are often banished by the families, forcing them into prostitution or begging to survive. There are close to 30 million widows in India.[4]

In Algeria, the Family Code of 1984 gave husbands the right to divorce their wives for any reason and ban them from their homes. Women in Algeria are now also threatened by death for not wearing a veil across the face. The Islamic fundamentalists have given orders to kill women who are not veiled and this has happened on a number of occasions.[5]

In Russia, nearly half the murder victims in 1995 were women murdered by their male partners.[6]

According to Jewish religious laws in Israel, a wife may not be given a divorce without her husband's consent.

Until 1991, beatings or murders of women by their mates were condoned in Brazil under "legitima defesa da honra." If the boyfriend or husband *suspected* his woman of adultery, he had the right to kill her and not suffer prosecution.[7] In Syria, a similar law is still valid.

In Peru, a wife can do business only with her husband's consent.

Islamic law condones polygamy, the practice of having multiple wives, and states that a woman must have a male "guardian" to leave the house.[8]

Seclusion, in which women are confined to their house or compound, is still practiced in many Muslim countries. This is a symbol of a man's high status and his financial wealth.[9] If a Muslim man wants a divorce, he just needs to state that intent, which is called *talaq*. Women are not given the option for divorce. In Pakistan, there is an Islamic ordinance that actually allows rape victims to be charged with adultery. *U.S. News & World Report* states that under this law there were approximately 2,000 women in jail.[10]

In Africa, including Egypt and the Sudan, 90 to 100 million women have had all or part of their vaginal labia and clitoris removed when they were young children in order to reduce their sexual desire and pleasure and to keep them virgins for their future husbands and faithful during the marriage.[11]

In Saudi Arabia and Kuwait, countries we sent our U.S. military to defend, women are denied freedom of speech, the right to vote, and even the right to drive. They are denied employment, education, and the right to travel without permission by a male relative. In Saudi Arabia, women must be segregated. It is the law.[12]

In Asia, female infanticide shows the preference for male children. One of the older methods of murder was feeding baby girls poisonous oleander berries. The new method of sex discrimination is to discover the sex of an unborn child through amniocentesis and, if female, to abort.[13]

"In almost every society and culture, boys are preferred and privileged over girls."[14] Higher male sex ratios in births have increased dramatically in countries like China, India, Pakistan, and South Korea recently. Couples are using amniocentesis and abortion to choose boys over girls. Smaller families tend to increase the preference for boys, as boys continue to have a higher economic value in many countries than girls.[15]

In India, girl children are fed last, fed only what is left. Men eat first. Thus more females then males die before their late thirties due to inadequate food and medical care.[16] Because of food taboos in Third World countries, where custom dictates that men eat first, then boys, and finally girls and women last, malnutrition is a major health problem for women. Harvard economist Amartya Sen calculates that 100 million women in the developing world are "missing," having died prematurely from the consequences of gender bias.[17] As Ruth Leger Sivard wrote: "Malnutrition remains a serious problem for women throughout the developing world. . . . The causes of malnutrition are many, ranging from inadequate food supply to food taboos and the physiological drain of child bearing, but another factor plays a key role: the inequitable distribution of food within the household. In the many regions of the world where girls are perceived as less valuable to the support of the family than boys, it is the boys who are given the more nourishing food. Men, too, are given the lion's share; the women in the household eat last and least."[18]

Some countries still prohibit women from using birth control. The United Nations reported that if all the women who wanted contraception were given freedom for family planning and birth control, there would be a 38 percent reduction in births and a 29 percent reduction in maternal deaths worldwide.[19] Pronatalist countries, countries that encourage reproduction for military or economic purposes, such as Kuwait, Chad, and Laos, limit contraceptives and choices for women, encouraging women to have male children to enlarge their military armies.[20]

As Marilyn French writes in her book *The War Against Women,* "Most countries try to regulate sexuality by regulating women." Women have been imprisoned, enslaved, or killed for losing their virginity, for adultery, or for prostitution, yet men are not punished for being the perpetrators or the clients. Countries withhold birth control from women, but condoms are not withheld from men.[21]

In Haiti, women were raped by soldiers, police, and other men in the military government of the early 1990s to politically repress their or their partner's participation in pro-democracy activities.[22]

In Rwanda's war massacres in 1994, a survey in the town of Rigali found that 15,700 women between the ages of thirteen and sixty-five had been raped.[23]

In Zimbabwe women are joining together to publicize the murder of women by men. The project is called the Femicide Register.[24]

In Taiwan, the civil codes, known as the Book of Family, prevent married women from rights of custody and divorce, property rights, and even the right of choice of where to live once married.[25]

In most countries, women cannot own land or share in owning the wealth acquired by their partnership with their husbands during their marriage. They have only their husband, father, brothers, or other male relative to depend upon, with no financial independence of their own. To survive, women are then forced to marry when they are deprived of land ownership rights.

The United Nations has found that there is "a global epidemic of violence against women."[26] All over the world, abuse of women in the home is rampant and very often condoned or enforced by customs, traditional roles, or law. Some 44 percent of Nicaraguan men regularly beat their wives or lovers. In the United States, every fifteen seconds of every day a woman or female child is beaten, attacked, molested, or raped.[27]

Everywhere women are worse off than men: women have less power, less autonomy, more work, less money, and more responsibility. Women everywhere have a smaller share of the pie; if the pie is very small (as in poor countries), women's share is smaller still. Women in rich countries have a higher standard of living than do women in poor countries, but nowhere are women equal to men.

TONI SEAGER and ANN OLSON,
Women in the World

The situation is indeed a strange one: We women look to men to care for and protect us, yet their gender is responsible for the majority of violence against us and our sisters throughout the world. The reality can feel overwhelming, but if we join with our sisters, we can begin the process of supporting one another in validating feminine energy and reclaiming our power to balance the global family.

14

Solutions Through Changing Our Fate

As women lead, they are changing leadership;
as they organize, they are changing organization. . . .
When women lead and articulate their purposes,
it seems to me that they work together not only as
individuals but with a sense of community and networking
in a healthy way. . . . Women have fresh and imaginative
skills of dialogue and are setting a more open,
flexible, and compassionate style of leadership.

MARY ROBINSON,
President of Ireland

Women Are Losing Power Globally

There are 191 countries in the world today, and the number of women in political positions of any stature is declining. There are only four women as heads of government, ten United Nations ambassadors, and seventeen speakers in parliaments. The United States ranks thirty-ninth in terms of female political leadership, with only 9 percent women in the Senate and 11 percent in the House of Representatives. We are losing our representation all around the world.

Changing the Balance

For planetary survival, we must first open our awareness to the rampant worldwide destruction and control of female energy. Feminine energy is the essence of our Mother Earth, who brings forth and nurtures all life. And it is this energy that connects all women, like sisters. When the power of the life-giving feminine energy is not honored with respect, or worse, when it is destroyed in any part of the world, this affects us all both physically and psychologically.

For example, feminine energy had no power or voice when husbands and adult children were sent to fight in Iraq in the Desert Storm conflict. Masculine energy was in control. Likewise, during the Vietnam War and the two World Wars, there were no female political or military leaders to create a balance in the decision-making process. These wars, as all other wars, were started and controlled by men in male-dominated governments.

Imagine what would have transpired if Iraqi, Vietnamese, German, and Japanese women, as well as American women, had had major influence and decision-making powers within their respective governments. History might have been different. There almost certainly would have been fewer wars. Families worldwide might not have been torn apart by the extreme losses brought on by these wars. And it can be different in the future. We are all connected to one another as women, and the powerlessness we have experienced around the world can be transformed into power as we seek to change the balance.

Until then, women's powerlessness perpetuates wars, because we don't have the authority to stop the territorial or economic aggressions before they begin. For example, what is taught to young girls in India, Asia, the Middle East, South America, and other developing countries about their self-esteem as women and their strengths or powerlessness will affect how they react to and influence the men who govern the systems that control their country's decisions about war or peace. This in turn will eventually affect you and your children living in the United States. At a minimum, you will pay higher taxes for military protection against escalating arms growth and more powerful Third World nations which are experimenting with and buying new weapons of aggression. At the worst, your sons and daughters, or their sons and daughters, will be sent to die in yet another war. Life on Earth is a web; we are all interconnected.

External Solutions: Gender Differences in Decision Making and Aggression

Women make decisions about conflict and war differently from men. This is in part because we are the birthers of our human species and have a greater stake in the continuation not only of our species but of other living species that are decimated by war and ecological destruction. It is a heavy burden to send your husband or your children or another's children to war. The mothers of these soldiers would weigh the decision of war much more heavily than the territorial male fighting to increase his power. As mentioned in the last chapter, the Cherokees and other tribes knew the importance of putting more women than men on their governing councils in order to balance the males' aggression.

There are many research studies that link the male hormone testosterone with aggressive behaviors and violence, and yet we let males run the world's governments unchecked and unbalanced. As Dr. Ann Campbell of Rutgers University points out: "Sex differences on the level of aggressive behavior have now been systematically observed in children from over a hundred societies around the world, documented in laboratories, seen on school playgrounds, and reported by teachers, parents and children themselves. That the male is the more violent is beyond dispute." On the other hand, Campbell cites research that has shown that women, even though they may be just as angry, seem to control their aggression better than men.[1] This is why we need to strengthen female energy worldwide in order to balance the masculine aggressive behavior and to allow women and men to work together as partners. But first we need the authority and power for men to respect us. Women from all parts of the world must understand that it does not benefit the entire species for men to rule alone.

The question then becomes, how can we assist our sisters in other countries to take on leadership roles, especially when their cultural heritage says it is taboo for them to make decisions outside of the home and family?

As always, education is the key since most societies' religions, customs, and traditions reinforce gender discrimination against women. That is why men are in power. Only ignorance continues to keep us from reevaluating these belief systems worldwide. In some countries, just giving women the knowledge that they do have rights is educational. In other countries, we can lend our experience and knowledge to women who are organizing and supporting the expansion of those rights.

The organization that has the diversity to put global ideas into effect is the United Nations, which represents worldwide member governments. In 1979, through the work of many women from many different countries, a document entitled the Convention on the Elimination of All Forms of Discrimination Against Women (CEDAW) was introduced and adopted by the United Nations. This treaty calls for the eradication of all forms of discrimination against women, including cultural and traditional discrimination. It encourages equality between men and women and realizes that the traditional roles need to change, with women taking more responsibility in society and men in the family. In addition CEDAW asks for government agreement, legislation, and implementation of equality for women and requires recommendations by a U.N. committee for those countries which do not take action. However, there is no punishment or disciplinary action for not following the recommendations of the committee.

CEDAW promotes the concept of positive discrimination until gender balance is a reality in governments. The key here is that, to achieve gender balance, women deserve and need a helping hand until they are no longer discriminated against. Brazil passed a law in 1996 requiring that at least 20 percent of all candidates for municipal office be women. So far, this is working, and at least 100,000 Brazilian women have run for office.[2]

Although CEDAW was adopted by the U.N., it had to be ratified by participating U.N. countries. In addition, countries were allowed to ratify the treaty with reservation, which meant they could disallow specific articles or paragraphs of the treaty. Since its adoption in 1979, over 130 countries have ratified CEDAW. Although this sounds like a positive development, too many countries have ratified the treaty with reservations. Most reservations concerning women's discrimination have been entered in the areas of family law, citizenship, and women's legal capacity.

Take a guess which countries have not yet ratified the CEDAW document? The United States of America has not, along with a number of other, mostly Third World, African, and Arab, countries. This is a travesty! Here in the United States, it is interesting to note that neither the Equal Rights Amendment for women nor the U.N. Convention on the Elimination of All Forms of Discrimination Against Women have been ratified. CEDAW was scheduled to be voted on by the Senate near the close of the 103rd Congress, but six Republican senators blocked the vote.[3]

What can we do to help ourselves and other women around the world?

We can write letters and postcards, we can phone, fax, e-mail, and telegram senators and congressional representatives calling on them to ratify CEDAW. They have had since 1979 to show their intentions. Remember, women are a majority, and we are the ones to put the pressure on for passage of these laws and treaties calling for an end to gender discrimination. We can use our vote together, the gender gap vote, to tell Congress that we have power as their constituents, whom they are supposed to represent, to demand our own equality—nationally with the ERA and internationally with CEDAW. It is incumbent upon us to balance the power for ourselves locally, nationally, and worldwide. As women, we must work towards having the respect and authority to make ourselves heard. All of us!

You can also let your governmental representatives know that you want them to give limited aid or support to countries where women have no voice in the affairs of government. Discourage our government from giving political backing or military aid to leaders who are not willing to include women in their administrations.

As mentioned in the last chapter, we can join women's local or global organizations. They need our ideas, our financial support, our membership, and our volunteer time. These groups need members to increase the importance of women's issues for lobbying power.

And, of course, we can affect the economy that drives the patriarchal system. Women, as the majority of consumers, can educate ourselves about the countries of origin of the products we buy. By including women's welfare in your buying and travel decisions, we can begin changing the system that seeks to dominate and control feminine energy.

Connection With the World of Women

No matter what country a woman lives in, her problems stem from the same source. Throughout different cultures worldwide, women lack equal status with men, and their work is grossly underpaid. Worldwide, women are fighting for contraception and safe, legal abortions so they can control their own bodies. Worldwide, violence and domestic abuse against women, as well as sexual exploitation, are rampant. Worldwide, women carry the burden of work within the home with little help from their spouses and partners, because it is deemed "women's work." Worldwide, women have very little representation in their governments but usually comprise the majority of the population. Worldwide, the average woman has little time for herself or the outside world—time that could be spent outside the home working on behalf of women's concerns, political causes, global inequities, and ecological issues. All over the world, women are struggling against not only an overabundance of masculine priorities, energy, and violence, but also a repressive attitude towards feminine energy. Yet worldwide, women have hope and are taking action, with courage and with heart.

In the Netherlands, women have pushed for equal pay, as well as a five-hour workday, so that their work outside the home and inside the home can be equally divided. In 1981, over 20,000 women went on strike to prevent new anti-abortion legislation from taking effect.[4] Among the striking tactics was the refusal of housewives to cook dinner.

In Peru, a group of women are fighting violence together in the shanytowns. If a woman is attacked or being beaten, she blows a whistle that she carries with her, and the other women, crowds of them, come immediately to the woman's defense.[5]

In Switzerland, women have signed petitions to demand a referendum amending the Constitution of Switzerland to require equal representation of women in federal positions of power.[6]

In Guyana, women have banded together as the Women's Rights campaign. In 1993 they presented a draft Domestic Violence Bill to the Senior Minister of Labor.[7]

A group of Scandinavian women are putting pressure on the United Nations to help redefine men's roles. They are trying to organize a U.N. conference entitled Changing the Role of Men: From Dominance to Partnership.[8]

In countries where sex tourism by males is big business and actually encouraged by the governments because it brings in foreign currency, some women are organizing to help the young girls who are the victims of forced prostitution. Women of the Philippines have started GABRIELA, and in Thailand women have organized the Women's Information Center. In Russia, individual women joined together to organize the All-Russia Women's Congress, which met in November 1994 to present resolutions to the Russian Parliament to eliminate discrimination against women and to promote equal rights.[9] Russian women deal with major sexual harassment in the workplace. Their lives are very difficult at this point in history.

As we learn about these and many more situations in which women take action to change the status quo of male domination, the question becomes: Why don't we hear any of these news items on radio or television? The answer is: *A dominant culture does not want a subordinate culture to receive encouragement or connection with one another to change or revolt.*

Yet the fact is, worldwide, from small neighborhood groups to large political coalitions, women are trying to make the future more egalitarian for their daughters and their granddaughters. We need to join them.

In fact, a very important event for women to connect with one another happened in 1995, when the Fourth United Nations Conference on Women was held in Beijing, China. These U.N. conferences set the tone for governmental attitudes and policies on women all over the globe.

The U.N. conference was organized so that there was a governmental conference attended by official leaders or delegates representing their country, while at the same time there was a parallel conference for "nongovernmental organizations" (NGOs) of women. There women's organizations and groups, both large and small, came from all over the world. Their purpose was to meet and work together to lobby and to put pressure on the governments to become aware of women's problems and discrimination and to share solutions. The NGOs also networked and put on cultural exhibits.

All individual women are welcomed and encouraged to attend these conferences. If you have a spirit of adventure, go to the next conference and make the difference.[10] You will make new friends from all over the world. But more important, you will be a significant contributor to change: It takes each one of us to move mountains.

Out of the work at the 1995 Beijing conference came an official document entitled "The Platform for Action," which is a guide for the actions governments can take to address women's status in their countries and the world. At the previous conference, held in Nairobi in 1985, governments *for the first time* acknowledged the horrendous problem of violence against women all around the world. These U.N. conferences are of utmost importance to women globally. Said Sarah Moten, of the National Council on Negro Women, who attended the Nairobi conference in 1985: "I can't even explain the spirituality that you felt, a commonality that women around the world are working for empowerment."

It is crucial that we continue to connect globally and work together as women. By doing so, we expand our sense of family. We have sisters around the world who affect our lives, just as we have an effect on their lives by the choices we make here in the United States. It is time to visualize ourselves as one big family, a family with much diversity, but a family nonetheless. We are a family that is in the process of balancing feminine and masculine energy, a family that is reviving feminine energies on the planet. To heal this planetary malady, we must think globally as sisters.

Women's Expression of Hope

There is an exciting event happening worldwide. Women all over the world are circulating and signing the Women's Peace Petition, which reads in part:

We are horrified at the levels of violence witnessed during this century and that women and children are the primary victims of war and poverty. On behalf of society at large, we, the undersigned women of the world, demand that annually, for the next five years, at least 5 percent of national military expenditures be redirected to health, education, and employment programmes. By doing so, one half billion dollars a day would be released worldwide for programs to improve living standards.

We also demand that war, like slavery, colonialism, and apartheid, be delegitimized as an acceptable form of social behaviour, and that governments and civil society together develop new institutions that do not resort to violence for the settlement of disputes.

Together, we commit ourselves, as half of the world's population, to use our power to ensure that these demands, which will promote international peace and security, are met through legislation and action. We resolve that we will inaugurate a new century that rejects warfare and promotes well-being, justice, and human rights.

This petition represents an opportunity for each one of us to join together as one of the family of women around the world. Already more than 100,000 signatures have been gathered. Please circulate or sign copies of this petition. Write to Peace Action International, 777 UN Plaza, New York, NY 10017, USA, or call (212) 750-5795 or fax (212) 867-7462. The petition will continue to be circulated through the year 2000 "as an expression of hope that the new millennium can be blessed by a culture of peace."

We are indeed poised on the edge of a new millennium—ruin behind us, no map before us, the taste of fear—and the hint of hope—on our tongues.

> *Yet we will leap.*
> *The exercise of imaging*
> *is an act of creation,*
> *is an exercise of will.*
> *All this is political. And possible.*
> *Believe it. . . . We are the women*
> *who will transform the world.*

From "A WOMAN'S CREED,"
Women's Environment & Development Organization

MEDITATION FOR CONNECTING GLOBALLY

Take five minutes now to do this visualization to set up a connection between yourself and other women and the Earth.

1. Sit down and relax. Let go. Every time a thought comes into your mind, just put it on a cloud and let it float away. There is a secret, and the secret is that your life has more meaning and breadth and purpose than you ever realized. You are here on Earth at this time because it is a very pivotal time for the rebirth of feminine energy and for the survival of the planet. Your energy and your purpose have been defined for you by your generation and by the conditions into which you were born. Trust that knowledge. And know that in this lifetime there are one or more things you can do to fulfill your obligation to your higher purpose, to life.

2. Now visualize the different countries. See the women in them. Connect with one woman in North America. Visualize

her life. Then one woman in Asia, then one woman in Europe, then one woman in Africa, then one woman in Latin America. Watch each of these women doing the same family work that you do. See them birthing, nurturing, cleaning, and going to their job. Connect with each one. Be in her heart so that you experience her struggles, which are your struggles as well. Visualize this, and connect to the energy of the feminine within us all.

3. Now expand your vision to picture Mother Earth, the planet, as one of us. Watch her birthing, nurturing, providing food, and caring and working for her family. See her birthing the plants, the animals, and the humans. Feel her providing water, air, food, fire, and beauty.

4. Now see the Earth's energy begin to connect you with the other women around the big circle, the globe. Feel with emotion the feminine, female energy becoming stronger and more connected. See that energy of the womb, of women exchanging, giving, and being given energy to and from Mother Earth. Feel, with deep emotion, this connection.

5. And now imagine all of us as one, within, providing our energies to change the world, to shift the consciousness, to save the planet, to save our home. See each one of us taking one or more actions to make this vision a reality. Feel millions of women connecting with you and contributing to this grand global healing—the healing of the feminine energy, the healing of the Earth. This global healing is the purpose in our time here in history, of our generations, of our lifetime here on the planet.

Many a humble soul will be amazed to find that the seed it sowed in weakness, in the dust of life, has blossomed into immortal flowers under the eye of the Lord.

HARRIET BEECHER STOWE

The women of Nicaragua have sent a profound message to the other women of Mother Earth. For many years they fought a war within their own country and became warriors. Now the Nicaraguan women are still fighting. But this time they are fighting for equality and integration, and for the Earth. "Compañeras everywhere on Planet Earth, we must remember that the struggle of women everywhere, like every popular movement, is the same struggle. The liberation of women will come about when women succeed in liberating themselves—and all society."[11]

To recapture the important points of this chapter:

1. Feminine energy has had no voice in the major wars of this century. It's time for women to be heard.

2. Education is key to ending gender discrimination against women. The U.N. Convention on the Elimination of All Forms of Discrimination Against Women (CEDAW) still needs U.S. ratification. Send a message to your legislators telling them to act now.

3. Join a women's local, national, or global organization.

4. Visualize yourself as part of one big family of women working together for change.

15

Awakening to the Crises
Facing Mother Earth

*Once again, [humanity] has failed to live by the divine
laws which we promised with our Creator to live by, and so,
gradually, the land and nature are getting out-of-balance.
Technology is rapidly eroding our ancient culture and tradition.
The wildlife and forest are diminishing rapidly, the precious
water and air are becoming unhealthy to drink and breathe.
Changing climate also is important to consider seriously
for it symbolizes a grave warning to [humanity].*

CAROLYN TAWANGYOWMA,
Sovereign Hopi Independent Nation[1]

Corporate Globalization Versus Mother Earth

In today's world, many multinational corporations are no-
madic organizations, paying male governments to degrade their
own countries. They are organized to move from one country to
the next in search of fresh resources, and to avoid environmental laws and regulations, as well as required humane working
conditions and salaries. Sometimes these very corporations present "greenwashing" commercials on television, telling you how
environmentally sensitive they are. "Greenwashing" is an environmental term used to describe tactics by corporations that

dupe the public into believing that their policies are environmentally sound and respect the Earth, her species, and human
resources when in fact they don't.

Driven by the greed for profit, these corporations are dis-
placing land owners in many countries, and pushing for unreg-
ulated production beyond what Mother Earth can sustain. The
Earth's nonrenewable resources are put on the auction block, for
sale to the highest bidders.

> *All over the world, indigenous peoples have been and are
> being systematically destroyed in the name of development.
> Languages are being eradicated, family relationships are being
> stretched and broken, traditional values belittled, and, as a
> last resort, genocide is being practiced. What is by now the
> well-oiled and finely tuned machine of the elimination of the
> indigenous people and thoughts has been practiced at least
> since the dawn of that day called Industrial Development.
> The global environmental crisis has more than adequately
> demonstrated that business as usual will not and cannot
> ensure global survival. What is needed is a fundamental shift
> in consciousness. This means that the views of indigenous
> peoples—our laws and rules and relationships to the natural
> world—have to be brought back into the picture. In fact, these
> natural laws and rules have to become the focus of humanity.*
>
> RUBY DUNSTAN, LYTTON INDIAN BAND,
> *Lil' Wat, Southwestern British Columbia*[2]

There is a true story that serves as an example of many other
instances of global destruction. This story is repeating itself around
the world in different countries, with different participants, human
as well as animals and plants. It is a story involving different governments and corporations; the destruction is the same.

Part of the story takes place in the West African country of
Nigeria—a country rich in oil, with half of its oil exports shipped

to the United States. In fact, you have probably fueled your own car at one time or another with gasoline derived from Nigerian oil. It has probably never entered your consciousness that your trip to the grocery store in your gasoline-powered vehicle has cost others their lives. But it has. Oil is like gold—according to the web page of the Union of Concerned Scientists, the United States spent $56 billion in 1996 importing foreign oil—and corporations and governments kill for it. The governments do the killing while the oil companies remain silent partners. The following story was reported in the *Los Angeles Times*.[3]

The oil exports from Nigeria have totaled $210 billion. The mega-corporations, Dutch Shell and U.S. Mobil, Chevron, and Texaco, have contracts with the male dictator government of Nigeria. But the Ogonis, an indigenous group of people, have been trying to stop the environmental destruction of their land, Ogoniland, by the oil companies. In return, they have received nothing but pain and death.

The subsequent grass-roots movement that is struggling for the survival of the Ogoni people has accused the government and Shell, along with other oil companies, of widespread killing and environmental damage. In turn, the government has executed the leaders of this group, calling them traitors. In fact, the government chose the day of the country's big football game to execute writer Ken Saro-Wiwa and eight others who were leaders of the Ogoni people's environmental movement. These are not the only deaths, just the latest. Hundreds of Ogonis have been killed for the oil, and the mega-corporations have been silent partners, looking the other way as the Nigerian government rids itself of the nuisance of people trying to save their land and homes.

As one resident told the *Times* reporter, "I saw women and children, mothers with babes in their arms, who were burned by soldiers. They burned them alive."

The oil companies know exactly what the government is doing to the people who owned the land until the oil was discovered. The oil corporations' silence is a form of compliance, and they are as guilty of murder as the male military government.

In 1997, several cities around the United States, including Berkeley, California, joined the Ogoni people's call for a boycott of Shell Oil and passed resolutions pledging not to use their financial resources to purchase or invest in anything related to Shell Oil, the major company involved in Nigeria. In this way, a new global consciousness may help the Ogoni people stand up to a huge corporation and save their part of Mother Earth.

Other fights like this are going on in places such as the Amazon, New Guinea, Australia, and even the United States, as indigenous peoples fight to save their land and themselves.

Most mega-corporations tend to view the Earth and its people as a resource for their economic profit. They have no soul.

What has been lost in all this economic corporate industrialization and its mechanistic view of Mother Earth and her children is the Earth's spiritual consciousness, her way of functioning as a whole, where everything is interconnected and depends on everything else. Women have also been lost and shoved into the background, where the feminine energy has been used as a resource to increase the power of the masculine energy. Unfortunately, without the balance of the feminine, the masculine is driving us towards destruction, towards planetary suicide, as we destroy the very home on which we live.

Let each of us open our eyes and take a look at what is happening to our Earth, our Mother, to Gaia.

The Awakening: Mother Earth Is Being Murdered

Before we can begin to make changes, first we have to know, in the simplest of terms, some basic truths about our planet, Gaia, and how she is being destroyed. As a water planet, she is very unique in that she is the only planet known to us that can sustain such a multitude of life and provide such abundance. We have taken this life-sustaining ability very much for granted. So involved are we in our work, our relationships, and our daily emotional drama, that we don't even think of our beautiful, mystical blue planet as home. But scientists have concluded that within our solar system, Earth is the only home humans will ever have to sustain us. Thus, we as women must break through our denial to see clearly what is being done to her and unite to save her.

Mother Earth, the feminine planet, is presumed to be approximately 4.6 billion years old. Yet in the last 100 years humans have done more to destroy the planet through human technological "progress" and industrialization than at any other time. Mass extinctions of plants and animals are occurring. There are thousands of species we will never see again. We are destroying millions of years of life expansion and evolution. There hasn't been a time of such mass extinctions on Earth since the demise of the dinosaurs. Soils are being poisoned and depleted. Our atmosphere, the very air we breathe and that protects us, is being poisoned. And if none of this awakens you, then be aware of the viruses that are being released and migrating north due to the destruction of the rain forest. Viruses such as Ebola and HIV are mutating before a cure can be found. What future do we have? And heaven help our children!

Is anyone thinking seven generations ahead?

Is anyone thinking one generation ahead?

Or are the mega-corporations merely thinking of next year's profits?

Humans Are Committing Suicide and Murdering Future Generations

Let's take a simple look at how the majority masculine leadership of governments and corporate global industries has affected our Earth.

The Atmosphere

The Earth is like the yolk of an egg. It is surrounded by the white of the egg, which is Earth's atmosphere, protected by its shell, which is the ozone layer.

In very simple terms, our planet lives in a great dark universe devoid of oxygen or life (that we know of). The atmosphere encompasses and protects the Earth from this dark universe. Everything we send up into the atmosphere, whether good or bad, comes back down to us in some form. You might say it's like "instant karma," a manifestation of the universal law of cause and effect.

Less than fifty miles wide around the Earth, the atmosphere contains gases such as carbon dioxide that are recycled to sustain life.[4] Much of the recycling of gases is done by trees and plants through a process called photosynthesis, which enables plants to live by absorbing the sunlight's energy and carbon dioxide as their food. The waste product of this process is oxygen, without which humans cannot live. This is why in the indigenous cultures, trees are seen as the "determiners" of energy. They can change one energy into another. Yet because everything is interconnected in some way, we humans do the same for the trees. When we inhale oxygen, we change it into carbon dioxide as we exhale. Humans, too, are "determiners" of energy, and we can choreograph our environment. But lately what we have been choreographing is destruction. The Native American Elders say that everything on Earth has an energy for a specific purpose—from the rocks, which are holders of energy, to the animals, which are receivers of energy. Everything is alive and vibrates an energy that is interconnected to another energy.

Global industry and the resulting convenience it produces, which we humans then overuse, are poisoning the atmosphere with gases that throw the life-sustaining gases in our atmosphere out of balance. In the last 100 years, over 64 percent of the increasing levels of one poisonous gas—carbon dioxide—has come from corporate industry.[5] This increase has set in motion many destructive reactions, such as global warming and the thinning of our protective shell, the ozone layer.

Global Warming Documented

Defined simply, global warming means that poisonous gases released into the air, mainly from industrial activities and the burning of fossil fuels as gasoline for transportation, are warming the protective atmosphere around the Earth. Thus, the average global temperature is rising. Climate expert Dr. James Hansen of NASA's Goddard Institute for Space Studies, who in 1988 warned the U.S. Senate Committee that the greenhouse effect had been detected, said that 1994 was one of the warmest years on record. The Institute also found the 1990s to be the warmest decade on record. Dr. Hansen also warned of future heat waves and drought. The National Weather Services' Climate Analysis Center reported the same, with the warmest March through December.[6] All ten of the warmest years on record have occurred in the last fifteen years.

Ross Gelbspan, in his book *The Heat Is On,* explains how disease is generated by global warming: "In 1993 a rodent-borne virus—hantavirus—broke out in the southwestern United States following a period of extreme changes in local climate. For six years the area had experienced a prolonged drought, during which the lack of water virtually eliminated the population of animals that prey on desert rats and mice—snakes, owls and coyotes. Then an unusually prolonged period of heavy rains in mid-1992 led to an explosion of pinion nuts and grasshoppers—both of which are nutritious rodent foods. In one year, the southwestern rodent population increased tenfold, in the process infecting the human inhabitants of the area."[7]

Gelbspan also reported that in July 1996 a panel from the World Health Organization, the World Meteorological Organization, and the United Nations Environmental Programme released a report warning that the impacts of climate change so threaten human health that "we do not have the usual option of seeking definitive empirical evidence before acting. A wait-and-see approach would be imprudent at best and nonsensical at worst."[8]

The most dangerous aspect of global warming is its effect on weather patterns, which cause catastrophes such as greater intensity of storms, such as hurricanes, and more severe droughts, record heat, intense rain and snowstorms leading to flooding, and forest fires. Climate variations affect agriculture with weather-reduced harvests and animal migrations, along with changes in water/ocean levels that affect shipping. There has been a dramatic rise in sea levels detected over the last several years. Massive flooding is a distinct danger. At an early Earth Summit + 5 meeting in June 1997, island nations appealed to world leaders to cut the emissions that lead to global warming. "Scientists predict that at the rate fossil fuels are being burned, spewing heat-trapping gases into the atmosphere, average sea levels could rise three feet by the year 2100. That would put 80 percent of the Indian Ocean archipelago under water," read one newspaper report of the Summit meeting.[9]

The Intergovernmental Panel on Climate Change (IPCC) was established by the World Meterological Organization and the United Nations Environment Programme to research and analyze current scientific, technical, and socioeconomic information concerning climate changes. In their 1995 assessment report of this data, they concluded that for the first time ever, increases in the global average temperature in the last century is "unlikely to be entirely natural in origin" and that "the balance of evidence suggests that there is a discernible human influence on global climate." They project an increase in average global temperature in the future. This assessment report received contributions and peer review from over 2,500 of the world's leading climate scientists, economists, and risk analysis experts.

More and more evidence validates the fact that El Niño weather patterns are increasing due to global warming and the increase in the temperature caused by human irresponsibility. Scientists have concluded, "Even though El Niños are a natural part of the Earth's climate, nature alone probably cannot explain the recent increases in their severity and length."[10] The conclusion seems to be that we will continue to see an increase in the frequency and intensity of El Niño storms.

Global warming is affecting food and water sources, as well as every ecosystem on this planet. In the past, climate changes have toppled whole civilizations. Hunger, starvation, and disease occur in direct relation to these crises. Again, everything is interconnected.

Ozone Depletion

There can be no life on this planet without our ozone shield. The ozone layer is a very thin shield of gases fifteen miles above the Earth's surface. It protects Mother Earth, like the shell of an egg, from the sun's ultraviolet rays. Without this protective layer, skin cancer, cataracts, and immune system disorders will increase. Climate will be affected. The basis of the marine food chain, plankton, is at risk. And ozone depletion also adds to the risk of global warming.

This may all sound like a *remote* concern for the future unless you happen to live in Australia, where one in three people will get or already have skin cancer. Or unless you live in Argentina, New Zealand, or Chile, which are closest to the monstrous ozone hole that opens every year over Antarctica from

September through November.[11] This hole is said to be as big as the entire United States.

In southern Chile there is a province, Ultima Esperanza (Last Hope), where it is said, "God stored all the beauty left over from Creation." But strange things are happening there. Again, everything in the natural world is interconnected. The birds and animals are getting confused. Geese breed in autumn, flamingos arrive early, and egrets fly around without instinctual migratory compasses. Many sheep and rabbits are going blind. Glaciers in Torees del Paines National Park are receding by 40 acres a year. In 1987, NASA sent 150 scientists and technicians 250 miles below the park to study the ozone hole and its effects. This was all kept very secret. The politicians and the governments, both here and there, kept very quiet. But the townspeople now say, "The Sky is sick."[12]

In April 1991, William K. Reilly, then Chief of the Environmental Protection Agency, said that the ozone over the United States was depleting 300 percent faster, and that it would lead to 200,000 more skin cancer deaths within the next fifty years.[13]

As the Elders say, when the masculine energies are out of balance, the Sun's rays become destructive to Mother Earth. The feminine suffers immeasurably.

Our Forests Are Being Massacred

Everyone talks about saving the forests, especially the rain forests, but why? Why are these greenbelts so important?

Plants are givers of energy. They give food, housing, oxygen, and beauty. As I mentioned earlier, Native American teachings explain that trees have an energy field around them. This energy field is very similar to a human being's. Trees are great choreographers of energy. They can transform negative energy into positive energy, just as they absorb carbon dioxide and change it into oxygen.

We think of the air around us as a limitless commodity that is fresh with every breath. Instead, it is a limited substance that is continually recycled and regenerated. According to Vice President Al Gore in his book *Earth in the Balance,* we are probably breathing recycled air that Jesus, Buddha, or Hitler once inhaled.[14] Air is recycled by the plants, the trees, and the forests, which serve as the lungs of our planet. The plants and the trees absorb the carbon dioxide and recycle it into oxygen, while we breathe the oxygen and exhale carbon dioxide. During its life span, one Douglas fir tree takes 400 tons of carbon out of the atmosphere by recycling and storing it.[15]

As the huge lungs encircling the Earth around the equator, the rain forests shelter over ten million species of plants and animals. In addition, there are thousands of healing substances from the rain forest that we will never discover because they have already been and are now being destroyed.

Some 25 percent of the world's healing drugs, which are plant extracts, come from the rain forest. Former President Reagan was saved from death during the surgery following the assassination attempt by a blood-pressure medication derived from the venom of the Amazon bush viper.[16]

The remission rate of childhood leukemia is now 95 percent due to a drug from the rosy periwinkle plant.[17] Yet 40 percent of the rain forests have been destroyed in just the last thirty years for greed and for profit, and out of ignorance and poverty. Norman Meyers, a British environmentalist, says of the rain forest and the extinction of its species: "If patterns persist, it may be the world's worst biological debacle since life's first emergence on the planet 3.6 billion years ago."[18]

Since we are putting more carbon into the air each year, can we humans even survive without this gigantic forest? In fact, according to the World Watch Institute, deforestation added about 1.1 to 3.6 billion tons of carbon dioxide into the atmosphere in

1994—carbon that increases global warming, since everything is interrelated.[19]

Forests of all kinds create and maintain our climate and our atmosphere. They actually create clouds of moisture, which then form rain clouds. Locally, the weather becomes hotter and drier as the forests are being cut down. Globally, deforestation increases global warming. The old forest destruction releases into the atmosphere the carbon that the trees have stored for us for years.

And yet in the United States, only 10 percent of the ancient forests are left.[20] Industrialization and development have ravaged the forests and ecosystems that they sustain. I will never forget the first time I saw a hill in Oregon that had been "clear-cut" by loggers. Every tree had been destroyed. Nothing lived, including the Pacific yew tree, which at the time was considered a trash tree without value. But today we know that the yew tree and women are very connected! The bark from this wonderful tree can help cure ovarian cancer. Seeing it trashed by the logging companies, I experienced a pain in my womb and in my heart. Mother Nature had not only been conquered, but massacred with chain saws. The lumber companies and the government call this "management," when, in fact, it is mass destruction. Once a forest is clear-cut, the whole bird and animal world of that forest is destroyed, along with all surrounding biodiversity. At least 45 species of animals make their homes in old growth Douglas fir trees, from the flying squirrel to the spotted owl.[21] If it hadn't been for the efforts of environmentalists to save the spotted owl, which lives in the same forests where yew trees grow, all the yew trees, women's womb trees, would have been destroyed by the logging companies as worthless. Women, the tree, and the owl; possibly it is synchronicity, possibly the Goddess at work. Everything is interconnected in Gaia's feminine web.

In May 1995, the *New York Times* reported that a Seattle, Washington, logging company recently bought 632,000 acres of forest in Chile. The logging firm, Trillium Company, was becoming another international nomad, blaming job losses on environmentalists, while in reality planning their move out of the country to seek cheaper land, trees, and labor.

In 1995, in another example of horrendous greed and political corruption, our male-majority government and corporate logging companies joined forces to clear-cut one of Alaska's largest temperate old-growth forests, paid for by the American taxpayer at a cost of $230 million. In essence, U.S. citizens were underwriting the death by starvation of thousands of Sitka black-tailed deer, bald eagles who nest in the huge trees, and grizzly bears, as well as the destruction of one of the oldest ancient forests. Its oldest trees, spruce and hemlock, date back to the sixteenth century, while other trees date back to the seventeenth and eighteenth centuries.

Since this is a clear example of how governments and corporations have colluded in our environmental catastrophe, let me explain how "the deal" between "the boys" came about. In Congress it's known as "pork." Eighty percent of the Tongass Forest is held by our National Forest Service, which is controlled by the federal government. Under a fifty-year contract, the government made a deal with the Alaskan and Ketchikan pulp companies to clear-cut the ancient forest. In return, the pulp companies pay $1 to $2 per giant ancient tree. But the U.S. Forest Service lost money big time because they had to build the logging roads through the forest and prepare the timber sales. In 1992, the Forest Service lost $64 million on the Tongass Forest contract.[22] In earlier years, from 1982 through 1987, $234 million was spent by the Forest Service on the Tongass "deal." The total income from the sale of these centuries-old trees has been less that $3 million for the U.S. Forest Service and our federal government.[23] In the meantime, you, the taxpayer, have paid to have your own ancient, beautiful forests destroyed, along with paying for the deaths of thousands of animals who made their home in these forests.

To add to the outrage, the majority of the lumber is being sold cheaply to Japan, and the only winners are the greedy men from the logging companies and the politicians who received donations to their campaign funds. All of them thought only in terms of the money that could be made in the present, while forgetting future generations as well as the exquisite wonder, beauty, and joy of the forests and all their living creatures. They have made decisions that are devastating to us, to our children, to the feminine energies, and to Mother Earth, all for money and masculine power. United States logging companies remain the number one most dangerous group behind deforestation as they devour forests throughout the world. They are becoming global.[24] The oxygen supply of the world is being threatened for the economic interests of a small group.

Viruses: The Earth's Immune System

The destruction of the ozone, which results in more ultraviolet light that suppresses the human immune system along with promoting global warming, will increase disease globally, and could play a part in the downfall of civilization as we know it if we don't change our current course.

Maybe it will only be out of self-interest that human beings stop destroying the Earth. As we forge into the unknown territory of the rain forests to exploit the bounty of the Earth's resources, we are unleashing monsters that we may not be able to control.

AIDS is caused by a virus that came out of the depths of the African forests, when a highway, the Kinshasa Highway, was built into the rain forests so the forest could be cut and developed. It was that very roadway that brought the HIV virus out of forests and into the world at large.[25]

Other viruses are also coming out of the wounded Earth, according to researcher and author Richard Preston: viruses like the deadly Marburg virus, Ebola Zaire, Ebola Sudan, and Reson; viruses like the Lassa Rift Valley virus, the Ryasanur forest brain virus, and Semliki forest agent, and many others. These viruses can travel through the human species in waves. And they are just twenty-four hours away by airplane to any major city in the world, just waiting to create a wave of death.[26]

Maybe Mother Earth will herself stop her human children from destroying her.

The Waters

The Kogi people live in the heart of the world, in Colombia's Sierra Nevada mountains. It is a small-scale microcosm of the entire Earth, with every conceivable kind of landscape and climate, from rain forest to Arctic-type snow peaks.

The Kogis, who call the humans in the rest of the world their "younger brothers," believe themselves to be the "elder brothers" for civilization, which predates the Spanish conquest. By not having contact with the rest of the world, they keep their culture and their community intact as it was hundreds of years ago. Only once have they contacted us, when they sent a message through the BBC to the "younger brothers" of the world. The message was that the Mother, the Earth, is dying. "Younger Brother thinks, 'Yes! Here I am! I know much about the Universe.' But this knowing is learning to destroy the world, to destroy everything. All Humanity."

Their message also said. "It is the mountains which make the waters, the rivers, and the clouds. If their trees are felled, they will not produce any more water."[27]

This is true! The water cycle includes the trees. Cutting down the trees—deforestation—can actually affect the rainfall in a given area, because forests attract and produce rain clouds, as well as store the water in their leaves. It is a simple formula: Clear-cutting of the land affects the amount of rain that falls on the land. Again, everything is interconnected and interdependent.

The Kogis also remind us: "The life of the water becomes the life of everything." Water is the sustainer of all life on the planet. Our own human bodies are made up of 71 percent water. We need to be in alignment with the waters for our own health. We cannot have sick waters without having sick humans.

Caring for our waters is caring for our own lives. Yet keeping our waters clean is one of the major problems we face.

Pesticides and Water

Pesticides used in agriculture to grow our food poison the groundwater when the chemicals run off the land and end up in our streams, rivers, and lakes. With over 800 million pounds of pesticides used in 1994, some 46 different kinds can now be found in the groundwater of 26 states. The National Academy of Sciences has connected pesticides and cancer deaths.[28] According to an Environmental Protection Agency survey, almost half of all American rivers, lakes, and creeks are still damaged or threatened by water pollution.[29]

Yet pesticides that are banned in the United States remain legal and are used in Mexico. One of the reasons the GATT treaty was so heavily lobbied by major corporations is that in Mexico the labor is cheap, in some places under $5 a day. In addition, the few environmental laws that exist are easily circumvented. Companies are moving to Mexico because they can make cheaper products, since they don't have to be concerned about either the environment or the people.

The water in Mexico is so bad from pesticides and sewage pollution that one river flowing from Nogales, Mexico, into Nogales, Arizona, brought hepatitis to that town at twenty times the national rate for American cities.[30] In fact, deaths caused by diseases from drinking polluted water in Third World countries numbers 25,000 people a day.

But is this just a Third World phenomenon?

After processing government records from 1983 to 1993, the National Resource Defense Council came to the finding that 53 million Americans, one in five, drank water with contaminants. They defined contaminants to include parasites, lead, pesticides, radiation, and bacteria. The federal government then issued a warning to the elderly and those with weakened immune systems, such as cancer or AIDS patients, that the tap water might be unsafe for them to drink. For example, cryptosporidium, which may be responsible for many gastrointestinal illnesses, is a dangerous parasite that chlorine doesn't kill. A Milwaukee treatment plant let the microbe escape in April 1993, sickening 400,000 people and killing 100. In Las Vegas in 1994, 30 people died from this same parasite.[31]

According to Professor James Symons, studies suggest increased cancer risk because chemicals and industrial pollutants, fertilizers, pesticides, toxins, and rusting underground tanks are seeping into underground water or flowing into streams and lakes.[32]

Shoshone Elder Corbin Harney says his people are pleading with us to join them in prayer: "Pray for the waters." The Native American grandmothers used to say, "The water said, 'If you don't take care of me, I can take life.'" Water is now doing just that around the globe, all due to humankind's negligence.[33]

The Ocean Waters

The waters teach us a great deal about our emotions and how we can approach life by flowing around obstacles. Have you ever been emotionally upset and sat by the ocean for solace? We are emotionally drawn to the ocean because water energy soothes our energies and our psyches. If we could learn to flow and give with our emotions as the waters do we would be more harmonious internally.

The oceans play an important role in our climate, absorbing the heat of the sun to cool Mother Earth. They also regulate our freshwater cycle through evaporation of the ocean waters into the atmosphere. This provides much of the planet's rainfall as the water returns to Earth to fill lakes, rivers, and streams.

Yet humans and our industries have used the ocean as our vast sewage and waste dump. There are over 1300 factories and 600 cities discharging over 5 trillion gallons of toxic wastes into the ocean yearly.[34] Every single day, millions of gallons of poisonous toxic materials and sewage, including virus and bacteria, are dumped into the oceans surrounding the United States alone.[35] Imagine what the figures must be worldwide! We are rapidly killing off much of marine life, and because the world's human population is growing at a phenomenal rate, the sick oceans can no longer sustain or provide the food that is the mainstay of many cultures' diets. Due to this pollution, as well as overfishing with heavy nets and equipment, the oceans are being poisoned and depleted of life. According to the Environmental Defense Fund, thirteen of the seventeen major ocean fishing grounds are in serious decline or fished out.[36]

In addition, our oceans are the last resting place for tons of nuclear waste, particularly from nuclear power plants that recycle the ocean waters to cool the reactors and then excrete the water back into the ocean. When humans consume the polluted radioactive fish, the radioactivity is absorbed through our stomach into our bloodstream, then into the different organs in our body. You don't have to have a nuclear reactor next door to be subject to this radioactivity. The currents carry pollution, and the fish swim for miles.[37] One of the most radioactive bodies of water, due to Britain's dumping of nuclear waste, is the Irish Sea.

Indigenous teachings say that the creatures in the oceans, the "swimmers," are receiver-givers of energy. They receive and absorb the energy of their environment, and they give it to those higher in the food chain that eat them. When you eat fish, you are eating what they have absorbed.

Swimming in the ocean waters can be dangerous to your health due to the pollution. When most people think of Malibu, California, they think of sun and surfing. But the pollution levels along the West Coast surf are rising rapidly. Bacteria levels are making people ill with flulike and respiratory-type symptoms.

For more than 50 years, my team and I have spent thousands of hours diving with aqua lungs and other underwater devices. I have seen with my own eyes how our waters have sickened. Reefs that teemed with fish only ten years ago are now almost lifeless. The ocean bottom has been raped by trawlers. Priceless wetlands have been destroyed by development. Everywhere there are sticky globs of oil, plastic refuse, and clouds of poisonous effluents. When we dump our wastes into our oceans and rivers, we are not "throwing them away." They return to us and our children with devastating impact through the food we eat, the water we drink, and the air we breathe.

JACQUES COUSTEAU

Wetlands

Wetlands are like the womb of Mother Earth—a place to birth and to grow. They serve as some of the Earth's most important ecosystems. They provide a breeding and growing area for over two-thirds of the fresh and saltwater fish and other sea creatures, birds, amphibians, and mammals. Wetlands are necessary to the survival of over one-third of North American bird species. Most all amphibians breed or live in wetlands. Wetlands also produce oxygen and prevent soil erosion and flooding.

Yet due to ignorance in the United States, federal and state governments have actually encouraged developers and farmers to drain wetlands. Some 91 percent of California wetlands have been destroyed in order to build developments.[38] All of this has been justified in the name of logical progress and development. But everything is interconnected. This patriarchal greed has come back to haunt us and will haunt our children and their children. The negative pole of male energy, in its need to try to control the feminine energies of Mother Nature and subordinate her, is killing her in a slow death. But Mother Nature will destroy us in the end, if we do not act quickly to balance the masculine energies, which define progress in terms of profits that can be gleaned from raping the Earth.

The Animals and Plants

What we have to do is to discover our kin, to discover our relatives who are the other animals and plants who are related to us through our Evolution and our DNA, because to know our kin is to come to love and cherish them.

PROFESSOR EDWARD O. WILSON,
Harvard University

Animals as Healers

On the medicine wheel, animals are seen as the receivers of energy. Not only do they teach us how to receive energy in order to balance ourselves and the Earth, but they also receive the energies of humans and the habitat in which they live. Animals bring balance to the energies of Mother Earth. Because animals absorb energy, they are healers. In fact, the Chinese use different animals for their energies to heal different diseases. In Native American medicine, the animals are called "sweet medicine" by the Elders, because their energy heals.

Yet the animal-human energy exchange is one of disgrace for humans and one of horror for animals. Even with the domestic pets we say we love, one animal is killed in our "shelters" every two to three seconds!

As teachers, each animal species carries a teaching of an archetypal energy. Therefore, watch the animals around you. They will teach you many things—how to survive, how to connect, how to nurture, how to let go, how to take what you need and know what to give back, and even how to know if you take too much.

For instance, coyotes teach us survival and how to deal with the daily tyrants in our life. They teach us how to be the gentle trickster and step into the light. They live in cities like Los Angeles and survive with their young. This is truly a feat.

Butterflies teach us about change, death, and transformation. Squirrels teach us about saving, and birds teach us to sing. The mountain lion teaches us to live alone with power. Thus each animal carries a teaching energy that will speak to those of us quiet enough to connect and to listen. Each animal speaks the language of adaptation, harmony, and balance—the language of nature.

In addition, each animal, including the human animal, perceives the world, its environment, through a different set of sensory perceptions. Snakes see and perceive infrared light. The wildebeest smells a human by the scent left on a buzzing fly.[39] Bees see ultraviolet light and perform a vibratory dance to direct other bees to a location. All of these creatures perceive the world in different ways, and yet all of them create balance.

In truth, science is discovering the interconnectedness and equality of each creature, all interdependent on one another for survival, including humans. When you are out in nature, you are in harmony. Don't you feel this in your heart?

Biodiversity and Prophecy

Many prophecies tell us that when humans turn to greed and destroy Mother Earth through the consumption of her body, her natural resources, the Earth Mother will in turn destroy us. And one of the first signs of this occurring, the prophecies predict, will be the strange behavior of the animals.

This is not just a random prophecy. It is a prophecy based on the animals being the receivers of energy in the Earth's system. They receive the energies of the natural environment, of humans, and of the environmental habitat created or destroyed around them. Thus, changes in animal behavior provides one of the first warning signs of dangerous ecological imbalances.

Over Chile, where the ozone layer has a hole in it every year, the animals are reacting and being affected. As mentioned earlier, they are losing their eyesight. They are also losing their radar, their sense of direction, of knowing which way to fly and migrate. Geese are breeding in the autumn, and the flamingos are arriving early in the season.[40]

In the Northern Hemisphere, the salmon are disappearing from the Northwest and Idaho's Salmon River. The cod are becoming extinct in Canada.

But the strangest occurrence was reported by the *Los Angeles Times* in 1994. It is the sexual confusion and reproductive defects that are appearing in animals all over the United States and throughout the world. The cause of this are the pollutants, such as pesticides and industrial chemicals that are flowing into the water, lakes, and streams from which the animals drink.

After studying the sea gulls on the California coast, Michael Fry, an avian toxicologist from the University of California at Davis, found the first evidence that pollutants in the environment were "feminizing" wildlife. There were more females than males because of the chemical neuterization of males.

Near Orlando, Florida, alligators are neither male nor female. Very few normal alligators can be found. Panthers are also on the list in Florida, as well as bald eagles in the Northwest, pallid sturgeons in the Missouri River, and osprey in Tennessee. And the list of animals, birds, and amphibians suffering from reproductive defects goes on around the world.

A group of twenty-one biologists sent out an unprecedented warning that government action is needed immediately in the United States. Among their comments:

> *When it's bad enough to scare us, it's bad. And when*
> *I sit down to think about this, it scares me stiff.*

> CHARLES FACEMIRE, *Toxicologist, Atlanta*
> *U.S. Fish & Wildlife Service*

> *If males aren't male and females aren't female, they cannot*
> *reproduce, and some outwardly healthy populations could be a*
> *generation away from extinction. Biologically, this is the most*
> *significant thing that could impair species and populations*
> *across the continent and across the globe.*

> TIMOTHY KUBIAK, *Chief of Contaminant Prevention,*
> *U.S. Fish & Wildlife Service*

Some of the chemicals, like DDT and PCB, are causing these effects decades after they were introduced. Remember when the chemical corporations told us they were safe and not to worry? You can buy some of the newer chemicals, which contain endocrine disrupters, at your local store. They don't harm the first

generation they come in contact with, but they afflict generations to follow. In fact, there are some suspicions by reproductive scientists that these chemicals might be causing reproductive
problems—infertility, breast and prostate cancers—in humans.[41]

As receivers of energy, animals—the sentinels as scientists call
them—are the first to alert us to environmental and human
health problems. One of the leading indicators of the Earth's environmental ill health is the disappearance of species. Out of
9,600 bird species, 6,600 species are on the decline, and over
1,000 species are nearly extinct. Amphibians such as frogs are
called "indicator species" by scientists. They signal problems in
the environment before they affect other animals, including humans. The thinning of the ozone layer has proven to be the cause
of the increased death and deformities among toads, salaman-
ders, and frogs. Some 90 percent of one kind of salamander's
embryos died or hatched with deformities. Researcher Dr.
Blaustein of the University of Oregon State warns, "Studies such
as this suggest that people should be concerned about a thinning
ozone layer and their subsequent increased exposure to UV-B radiation."[42] According to famous Harvard scientist and biologist
E. O. Wilson, over 50,000 species a year are becoming extinct.
That is five species an hour.[43] Unfortunately, we have no idea
how this will affect the human species or what this will do to the
web of life that supports us.

Ecosystems and the Ripple Effect

Ecosystems sustain the family of animals, plants, and organ-
isms that live in one area, interdependent on one another for
food, for interspecies sewage disposal, and for species continuation. In short, ecosystems sustain life.

Remove one important animal, and the whole ecosystem
changes. For every mammal species that becomes extinct, 200

other animals and possibly 70 plants will disappear as well.[44] This is what scientists call a "ripple effect." There is a web of life, not just separate parts.

For instance, on the Barro Colorado Island, the extinction of the large predators, pumas, eagles, and jaguars caused the whole island to change. Why? Because the big predators used to eat the medium-sized predators, who ate the birds and their eggs or the seeds of trees. When the pumas and eagles disappeared, the medium-sized predators grew in population, demolishing the bird populations, as well as eating the seeds that fell on the ground to grow and become the larger trees. Therefore, only the smaller plants have grown, which is expected to cause a population shift to mice and rats.[45]

In his book *The Third Chimpanzee,* Jared Diamond writes that there are "four mechanisms—overhunting, (foreign) species introduction, habitat destruction, and ripple effects," which will probably cause over half of the existing species of birds and animals to become extinct or endangered by the middle of the next century.[46] What a legacy to leave our children and their children. Today's parents should be ashamed of this environmental inheritance we are leaving our children.

When are we going to wake up to what the present and past male-dominated governments and corporations are allowing and doing to life on Earth? Birds, plants, and animal species are losing their habitats and becoming extinct because we humans are poisoning and destroying the natural world for profit and convenience.

We are building concrete cities over the Earth's womb area, the wetlands, where young are bred and nurtured. We are building freeways into the rain forest and housing tracts in meadows or canyons, destroying thousands of species and their homes. By the end of the century, just a few years away, there will only be four large untouched tracks of wilderness left anywhere on Earth. In addition, men are hunting animals to extinction for fun and for sport, or for parts of their bodies—such as ivory from the elephants or fur from the large cats to adorn women's bodies. The illegal wildlife trade, black-market animal body parts, is estimated to be $2 billion to $3 billion a year. Only drugs and weapons are more profitable illegally.[47]

We seem to have lost all reverence for life forms and their habitats.

What difference does this make? As you have read, humans, too, are an interdependent species, dependent on other living forms for our food, oxygen, clean water, and shelter—for our very survival. Everything comes from the natural world. And we are forgetting this, because most of us live in cement communities.

Yet science is continually discovering and rediscovering the interconnectedness and equality of each creature, as well as the interdependence on one another for survival, including humans. When you are out in nature, don't you feel this in your solar plexus?

Will Earth Changes Affect You?

How often do we read about the crises affecting Mother Earth and then go on with our day-to-day lives, forgetting the emotions we felt and the actions we promised ourselves we'd take? I hope that after reading the material in this chapter, you'll keep the information alive and present within you as you begin to put into practice the solutions outlined in the next chapter. Before ending this chapter, I'd like you consider several questions which I think will help you decide how much meaning this knowledge has in relation to your life. These are simple questions that came out of the Second Morelias Symposium held in Morelias, Mexico, in 1994. This gathering brought together scientists, poets, population biologists, environmentalists, and humanists to discuss the fate of the planet.

1. How can we consider environmental protection to be a luxury?

2. What will happen if we continue to insist on dominance instead of balance at the expense of every other species?

3. Will the children of the next century see a monarch butterfly, a tiger, a grizzly bear, a rock in the forest in the Malaysian borneo, in Mexico's wilderness, or anywhere in West Africa?

4. Why is the production of a machine gun treated as economically desirable while cleaning a river from which people must drink considered a costly extravagance?

5. How realistic are official environmental policies that ignore the overconsumption and population crisis?

6. What will our money be worth when we have turned the Earth into a wasteland?

7. Do you think these questions have anything to do with YOU? If so, what can you do about that? How do we draw each other out of complacency?

What can you do to address the issues raised in this chapter and this book? We are one of the last generations of women that has the chance to make some very important decisions for our future and for generations to come. But we must have the power to balance the male energy and channel it into a more positive, survival-oriented, less greed-for-now direction. It is absolutely necessary that we take action now—for our children's future and for every plant and animal living on Mother Earth.

In the 1960s, women of the Aquarian Age began changing the power structure of American society. Yes, the changes mean that we are working harder and changing roles, but this is the beginning of the shifting of power, of the balancing of energies. We are being forced in our everyday lives to take our power, to be independent, and to face our fears. The generations that are born in a time of transition, when power is shifting, become the very catalyst of that shift. We, the women of today, the women who carry the feminine power of our time, will either save the Earth or ignore this crisis to our peril.

16

Solutions:
Our Role as Women
in Saving Life on Earth

We must all see ourselves as part of this Earth, not as an
enemy from the outside who tries to impose his will on it.
We, who know the meaning of the pipe, also know
that, being a living part of the Earth, we cannot
harm any part of her without hurting ourselves.

LAME DEER

Internal Solutions:
Nature Is the Healer of Feminine Energy

You may have found the last chapter painful to read; I know
I found it painful to write. What we have done to planet Earth
under our male-dominated system is truly horrifying. Yet we still
have cause for great optimism and hope.

Nature is our great healer. When we connect with her, her
spirit heals our energy and quiets our mind. She brings us back
into alignment with our spiritual self. She reawakens our connection to our soul. For it is in nature that we find the cycles
of universal energy that mirror the cycles of our lives—from
birthing to living to dying. In nature, we as women can heal our

overstressed and depleted energy systems. Mother Earth is alive with her revitalizing feminine energy.

In the city, we become robots. We cannot connect or heal surrounded by concrete and asphalt environments. The energy there is not alive. Because concrete buildings and asphalt streets separate us from the Earth's energy, the life force becomes stressed and negative, bouncing from one human being to another. Negative energy cannot be absorbed or changed when there are not enough healing, living energies, such as plants, trees, or animals nearby. But when we are surrounded by nature, everything is vital and alive. Trees, plants, animals, and insects absorb and choreograph our energy and the energy around us for maximum efficiency. This great power of nature is why we feel so much better after a day in the mountains, by a stream, or in the countryside.

Go into nature. Spend time sitting on the soil, the Earth's skin, or leaning against a tree watching her children, the animals. Slow down to the vibration of the surroundings and align yourself with the energies of the natural world. You will be healed as she absorbs your negative, stressful energy and replenishes it with harmony and vibrancy. Everything in nature is birthed from the feminine energy. Look around you and see that power. Align with her.

To regain your inner strength, your inner wisdom, and your magic, you can reconnect with the great spirit/being Gaia. She has been waiting for you to return to her and regain your power to sustain yourself and the feminine energies. To begin, we must attune our energy to her cycle and hear the voices of her children, all her children—the elements like air and water, and plants, animals, and birds.

"Everything is born of the feminine." Encode this message into your consciousness. Let it ring in your ears; let it be your mantra. For in that one sentence lies the magic of the web of life, of nature, of Gaia.

You are her. She is you. Remember that always!

Our true purpose for being a human is to bring beauty to the world, and if we are to do that we have to look at beauty itself, which is the Earth, and see what she does and then learn to do that ourselves. That is to live impeccably.

THUNDER STRIKES

TREE MEDITATION

The tree meditation is an old meditation and visualization from the yogic tradition to balance the feminine and masculine energies. It also reconnects us with the roots of the feminine energy.

1. Find a tree out in nature that attracts you. If you don't live in a rural area, use a tree in your yard or one in a local park, preferably in a quiet spot. It is important that you do this on the ground, connected with the Earth. While doing the meditation, be aware of a sense of bonding and relationship with the Earth as your mother who feeds you, clothes you, and sustains you.

2. Lean your back against the trunk of the tree. Breathe deeply. Inhale slowly to the count of four, then hold to the count of four, and finally exhale to the count of four. Each time you inhale, visualize taking in inner strength, wisdom, and love. With each exhalation, release your fears. Do this until you feel peaceful.

3. Now imagine yourself as the tree—the tree of life. Extend your arms above your head and visualize your energy reaching and stretching through the branches toward Father Sky. Inhale to the count of four as you do so. Hold to a count of four. Then exhale to the count of four, bringing your arms down into a relaxed or meditative position

and letting the energy of Father Sky flow back through you. Rest.

4. Now visualize the roots of the tree below you. They go deep down into Mother Earth to absorb the energy of the Earth. Inhale to the count of four, ground yourself, and feel your roots go down deep into the Earth alongside the roots of the tree. Hold to a count of four, visualizing the strength of feminine energy, all the mother energy of the Earth, filling your body. Then exhale, and as you do, release any fears or tension. Rest and relax.

5. Then, to the count of four, breathe in both energies simultaneously — the masculine energy of the Sun and the feminine energy of the Earth. Hold to the count of four. Visualize the masculine energies flowing down through the branches and the feminine energies flowing up through the roots into your sacred body, then blending in balance and harmony. Exhale to the count of four, letting go of any remaining imbalance. Sit still for several minutes as your energy balances and transforms.

FLOWERING TREE CEREMONY

This ceremony comes from native spiritual traditions and offers another very effective way of balancing your energy, particularly meeting the needs of your inner child by allowing you to connect with the plant world. You can do this ceremony as often as necessary.

1. Go into nature and find a tree that attracts you. Again, if you do not live in a rural area, a tree in your backyard or in a local park will do. Find the largest tree you can. Ask the tree if it is willing for you to perform a ceremony with it. Press your body against the trunk if you can, or at least place your hands on it. Very quietly feel the energy.

Does it feel welcoming? if you do not feel any connection, find another tree. If the energy of the tree resonates with you, walk around it three times clockwise, then sit with your back to the tree, facing South.

2. Close your eyes and relax into a meditative space. As you sit facing South, ask this question: "Who am I?" Still the mental chatter as best you can, and open yourself as an empty cup to receive whatever may come to you. You will not necessarily get an answer through your mind in the form of a mental idea; insights and answers may come to you as bodily feelings, shifts in your energy, or as emotional energy. Take your time, and as insights or new understandings come to you in answer to the question, accept them without judgment. You may simply put them in your memory bank, or you may jot them down on a pad of paper.

3. When you feel complete, move clockwise to the West and ask, "Where did I come from?" Repeat the same process as in the South.

4. Move clockwise to the North and ask, "Why am I here?" Again, repeat the same steps.

5. Move clockwise to the East and ask, "Where do I go from here?" Repeat the same steps.

6. When you feel complete in the East, get up and walk around the tree clockwise, to the direction that felt the most significant to you, the direction that gave you the most insights and illuminations. Hug the tree, placing your body fully against its trunk. Breathe deeply and align your energy with the tree.

7. Begin to perform "give-aways." For example, "Great Spirit [God/Sacred Universe/Universal Spirit/or whatever word you use to describe the Divine for yourself], I have seen that my jealousy for my sister has shut me down and

closed my heart. I give that away now!" Or "Great Spirit, I have felt how much I dislike my job and how my lack of confidence keeps me stuck there. I give that away now!" Continue your give-aways until you feel clear and complete. If you do this with sincerity and power, you will feel the energy shift from you into the tree, The tree, being in natural balance and alignment, will absorb and transform the negative energy without any harm to itself.

8. Thank the tree for allowing you to perform a ceremony with it, and leave it with a gift. This can be some loose tobacco or finely ground cornmeal (both of which are sacred in native traditions) or a strand of your hair. These symbolize your gratitude, your respect, and your honoring of the tree's gift to you. The ceremony is complete. Walk away from the tree, and take your cleansed and balanced energy, your new insights and understandings, with you as life enrichments.

With over 150 million women in the United States, if even 10 million women did one or the other of these energy balancing meditations once a day, there would always be women simultaneously working together in a connected way to balance feminine and masculine energies.

After all, women are the changers of energy through our power to transform energy. We live in our upper energy centers—heart, communication, and spirit—and it is through the power of love that we birth men into these higher energy centers. And with the energy of intent, we can do that through this meditation. It is our magic as women to birth both physically and spiritually, and now we need to rebirth ourselves in our power and connection to one another and to the Earth, Gaia, so that we can spiritually transform the balance of masculine-feminine energies.

Visions of a Spiritual Awakening

As many scientists and spiritual leaders are predicting, it will require a great awakening, a spiritual awakening, to save our home planet from further destruction and death. Yet the ability to bring about this awakening lives within each one of us. Because the female process is one of spiritual connection, of cycles, of interconnectedness to relationships, nurturing, community, and the divine, we are ideally suited for this role.

If we want to achieve anything worthwhile, all we have to do is get women together and we will do it—whether that's stopping drunk drivers, saving children, feeding the homeless, or saving the world. We can do it because our passion comes from the heart, and because we know how to feel and think from our heart, from our head, and from our womb.

As women, we must begin to use these characteristics to balance the preponderance of logical, objective, left-brained *head-dominated* thinking, which has disconnected us from the Earth and her children. The masculine stance of conquering Mother Earth and nature solely for humankind's own purposes has placed the entire planet in jeopardy. War against Earth and nature has been a war against feminine energy. Let us begin envisioning an end to this war.

As I sit here writing these words to you, I envision millions of women awakening, before it is too late, and doing just one thing each week to help the children, the animals, the future of our planet Earth.

I envision women banding together to save precious open space in their local communities.

I envision women's groups connecting with environmental groups to stop the industrial pollution that is blackening our air, causing acid rain, polluting our waters, and giving cancer to our children and families.

I envision millions of women waking up and taking our power, empowering ourselves and one another, working together globally for one another and the environment. This is happening already, and it will continue to grow.

Hold this vision with me every day, and it will become a reality. If anyone can do it, women can. And we know it!

External Solutions: Acts of Power

*Where large sums of money are concerned,
it is advisable to trust nobody.*

AGATHA CHRISTIE

The time for action is now. We each need to choose to focus on at least one aspect or solution and move forward quickly. If each woman in the United Sates would choose to take one positive action a week, women could accomplish over 100 million actions a week to save the planet. That alone would turn the dangerous tide of destruction. Do you realize the tremendous power we can have when we join together?

First and foremost, the solution cannot remain primarily a political issue, because we cannot depend on politicians to solve these problems for us. Politicians cannot generally take the high road on environmental issues, because many of their campaigns are funded by special interest groups that put net profits before global health and sustainability. We need to understand that true change is up to us. The multinational corporations pour millions of dollars into lobbying our politicians, deny that any ecological problems exist, and influence them to vote against environmental solutions, which might hurt their profits.

As an example, consider the tobacco industry. Large campaign contributions supported congressional representatives voting for large government subsidies that protect the tobacco industry. The Philip Morris Company in 1995–1996 donated approximately $4 million dollars to federal candidates.[1]

Oil and gas interests have contributed over $53 million this decade to politicians and their parties, according to Greenpeace. This money carries an obligation. These companies want power, influence, and votes in Washington, and politicians owe them that obligation. The large oil companies have spent millions trying to tell us that global warming doesn't exist. They have funded scientists who are willing to validate that propaganda in exchange for large research grants and other perks. They also spend millions on "greenwashing" commercials on television.

We cannot afford to put our trust in many politicians. Most politicians are reactors; they don't initiate the energy. Like the tobacco industry itself, many of them have no conscience. Only very focused and concerted public interest and activism can move Washington in the face of all this.

Because we cannot count on our government representatives to see clearly and to act with complete integrity, we must take responsibility for ourselves and our planet if we plan to survive into the next century. Our actions today will affect generations of our children to come—our daughters and sons and their children.

Take Action: Global Warming

Pressure Your Representatives

Put pressure on your federal, state, and local governments to cut industrial emissions. Write to federal agencies if you think that a company in your area is not following fair guidelines.

Write to the president and Congress to urge them to sign environmental treaties. Our elected officials have been reticent to be leaders in the environmental arena, even though our country causes a disproportionate amount of pollution. These politicians fear taking action that might cut corporate profits—and their campaign contributions. We need to let them know that voters realize the magnitude of this crisis and want immediate action.

In America there are over 140 million cars, which account for 13 percent (700 million tons) of the total carbon dioxide emissions worldwide, a major cause of global warming. According to the Ozone Action Website, the United States alone is responsible for 23 percent of the world's greenhouse gas emissions.

Obviously, ride sharing, bicycling, taking public transportation, and walking are the best options. But in many cities this is difficult. According to the Union of Concerned Scientists, one of the most important actions we can take to slow global warming is to buy a vehicle that is highly fuel efficient. One gallon of gasoline creates 20 pounds of carbon dioxide in the atmosphere. Choose a car that makes that one gallon travel a long way. If you are going to use your car, drive at a steady pace, which reduces gas consumption. Use the air conditioner as little as possible, since air conditioners use chlorofluorocarbons, which affect the ozone layer. Use radial tires, which increase your gas mileage. Cut down on extra trips to the grocery store or other destinations. Organize your driving miles to minimize gasoline use.

To solve global warming from another angle, do what you can to help save trees and forests, the lungs of the world. Trees also stop soil erosion, which creates famine. Trees regulate rainfall and climate, absorb carbon dioxide, and store it. Fight for the trees for they are breathing and transforming the poison. Join environmental organizations that are fighting for the rain forests and other forests of the world. Contribute financially, and also volunteer your time. Recycle paper products and purchase products with a minimum of packaging. Use wood sparingly in construction; investigate alternative building materials. Participate in tree-planting campaigns.

At the time of this book's writing, the Pacific Lumber Company has negotiated a deal with the U.S. government to cut and log some of the last stands of old growth redwood forests in northern California. These trees were here when the Spanish explorers first arrived. They belong to our children and their children. Each old growth tree has stored and recycled at least 400 tons of carbon dioxide during its lifetime, some of which will be released into the air when the tree is cut down. Multiply that by 200,000 acres of trees. Pacific Lumber is looking forward to $150,000 of profit per old growth tree, despite the fact that it is irreplaceable.[2] We have a short time to save these and other forests. Call the Sierra Club immediately to get involved. Write to the governor of California and to your senators. Put major pressure on politicians, for they should be representing you and not their campaign contributors. Let us show our strength and save this old growth forest for our grandchildren.

We Are the Birthers of the Earth

Among the many problems we face, overpopulation is one of the more devastating. There are too many people on this planet consuming too much of the Earth's resources. Everything we use comes from Mother Earth—from our houses to our food to our clothes, our cars, and our computers, and all the luxuries and conveniences advertisers have convinced us we can't do without. Mother Earth can only sustain a maximum number of humans, particularly humans who only take from the Earth and give nothing back.

According to the natural law of reciprocity, there must always be an exchange of energy to keep things alive. This creates an intimate interdependence among all things, a divine exchange of energies. We humans have not been in reciprocity with Mother Earth for a very long time. There are too many of us just taking energy from her. We need to decrease the birth rate until we can balance this energy exchange. We have overproduced ourselves and are continuing to do so. There are now over 5 billion people on the Earth, and that number will double in the next eleven years if we don't do something.

With a population of over a quarter of a billion people, we think of the United States as having our numbers under control. Yet Americans consume at least five times as much per person as people in most other countries. Each child we birth is equal to five children birthed to a woman in Peru, in terms of resource consumption.

Women can have a great impact on the population explosion if we are responsible today for the number of children we birth. We have the power to choose. Don't let anyone take that power away. If we replace only ourselves and our partner, we can ensure a sustainable future for those children. More than two children per couple, and the population continues to explode and uses more resources, placing the Earth in great jeopardy.

Additionally, the more education women have, the fewer children we tend to birth because we are able to express ourselves creatively in different areas. We also give smaller families more quality time and a better lifestyle and education.

The Oceans and the Waters

What can you do to help? Join an environmental group. If possible, donate your time as well as whatever money you can afford. Choose a body of water—a lake, river, stream, or ocean in your area—and join with others to help protect it. Write to your legislators to set limits on industrial waste dumping into rivers, lakes, and oceans. These bodies of water are not garbage or chemical disposal dumps.

Safe drinking water is becoming a scarce commodity. What you pour down your kitchen sink might return to you after being processed by your local water treatment plant. So be careful what you are discarding. Don't throw paint or oil down storm drains, which often drain to the nearest bay, lake, or other body of water. Avoid using heavy pesticides or fertilizers on your lawn and garden, which may drain into storm drains and ultimately kill hundreds of fish. Remember that what drains from your washing machine also becomes pollution. If you do just one thing for the Earth and the future of our children, buy dish and laundry detergents that are phosphate-free.

Use water with awareness. The average person in America uses 60 gallons of water a day; at least 24 of those gallons are used carelessly. Conserve water; it might be you who needs it in the future. Fresh water is not an endless commodity. Many Americans now buy purified drinking water for this very reason. The safety of tap water has become questionable.

Pray for the waters. The Elders say that water holds the emotions and spirit of the Universe. Water is used in almost every religion in some ceremony or ritual. Say a daily prayer for the waters to heal, and do whatever you can to help the waters in your part of the Earth. Water is sacred; it is the blood of Mother Earth.

The Animals

In the words of the Great Spirit: Look around you,
my daughters and sons, at the insects, animals, plants,
and trees of the forests and fields; at the fishes and waters;
at the birds and the air; and know that they do not need
you to survive. Rather, it is you who need them! Therefore,
treat all beings, all things which I have made for my
purpose, gently, with love and compassion: respect them
as if they were yourself. Only then can you be free,
for truly, you are all my children.

BILLY MICUS

As I wrote earlier, animals are the receivers of energy. Many Elders say that animals are "sweet medicine," because they teach of the sweetness of life. Through their behavior, animals carry an archetypal energy that reflects back to us a mirror of what we need to learn about that energy. When we understand the different animal energies, we can gain knowledge and strength about ourselves and our actions or reactions in the world.

The Balancers of Nature

All species are intimately interconnected and interrelated. We humans are an integral part of this magnificent matrix of life, which makes possible our existence as well as our ability to evolve. At some point we have to wake up to the incredible arrogance of the idea that we can prosper and evolve apart from the richness of our relationship with all life.

Animals are the balancers of the natural world, and as such provide a wonderful service to us. Without coyotes, snakes, or owls, rats and mice become rampant and cause human diseases. The smaller animals are gauges of how safe the world is to live in. They are the first ones to die in places where there are too many toxins. This warns us that our environment is becoming toxic. Animals species are being killed, and their homes are being destroyed by logging, development, global warming, ozone depletion, pesticides, highways, and so forth.

Congress in 1998 contains many extreme right-wing Republican senators and representatives who are attempting to undermine the Endangered Species Act. They represent oil, gas, timber, and mining industries. They call their efforts to tamper with the Endangered Species Act the "wise-use movement." The Endangered Species Act is the only protection dying species have between them and extinction. Call or write the president and your congressional representatives to tell them how important the Endangered Species

Act is to you. Educate yourself about this act and other bills that are being considered in Congress to support or undermine the Endangered Species Act. (The organization Defenders of Wildlife would have this information on hand.) The animals need your help! We are losing thousands of species, never to be seen again on this planet. Remember how the Endangered Species Act helped save the spotted owl? When habitat was preserved to save the spotted owl, many other animals who made their home there were also saved. Saving the spotted owl also helped save yew trees, which are now saving women's lives in the treatment of ovarian cancer. Everything is interconnected.

As I write this book, it is the Chinese year of the Tiger, and yet the tiger is fighting for its very survival as a species. The population of these beautiful creatures has dwindled by 95 percent, so that there are fewer than 6,000 tigers left in the world today. In their natural habitat, the big cats are the balancers. They keep all other species in balance. We can't afford to lose them. The World Wildlife Fund, the National Geographic Society, and the Wildlife Conservation Society have joined together to try to get you involved in saving the tiger. Call one of these organizations and help them with time or money.

We humans always have particular animals that resonate with our energy. Consider helping the animal that you have been most attracted to in this lifetime. It might be a bird species, elephants, the big cats, or the wolves. Each species is in desperate need of your help. There are many organizations to channel your energies. This can give you a sense of strength as you start helping instead of remaining helpless.

In your local area, there may be a species that is threatened with extinction. Find out about that species by calling one of the environmental organizations or university ecology departments. Start making changes in the environment to help that animal. The actor Eddie Albert chose the huge pelican in California, and his activism helped save the species from extinction. Such work will also help you heal. If each one of us started saving one animal species, we could save all of them for our children. Make it a project for your family. This is the world your children will inherit, and they need to start learning about saving it. We must pass this lesson on from one generation to the next.

Local Groups

Never doubt that a small group of thoughtful,
committed citizens can change the world;
indeed, it is the only thing that ever has.

MARGARET MEAD

There are so many choices available to us to help balance the male-female energies and restore a sense of value, honor, and sacredness to Mother Earth and all her children. I see women who are lonely and want companionship, but to attract we have to be charismatic and have a purpose and an energy for life. Without the passion to risk and to get involved and to change our environment, we will all eventually perish. It is as simple as that! Get out in the world, my sisters, and act! Forget the laundry, and do something you will be remembered for. Stop the waiting.

Join a local environmental group. Every city or town, large or small, is fighting to preserve some part of the natural environment. In the small California town of Lompoc, one of the industries has been releasing toxic sulphur dioxide (SO_2) on the weekends when the air quality control office is closed. And the farmers have been using so many pesticides that the hospital is reporting higher cancer rates and more respiratory disorders. The citizens have joined together to fight to save their town. To heal a place that you love is a grand accomplishment. It also brings healing to the healer.

Spend actual time in the natural area you are trying to save so you can fill your soul with the energy of the area and the real meaning and depth of what you are trying to accomplish. Remember, you are not alone. You are connected with the feminine energies of other women all over the planet, and the feminine energies of nature will give you strength.

National and International Groups

Why join a national environmental organization? Besides the fact that all of the organizations need funding, volunteers, and equipment to continue their mission, it is very important that these groups have very large memberships to give them the power and influence they need to pressure politicians into saving the animals and the environment. With large memberships, they can let the politicians know that many of us, their voting public, fully support the environmental movement. As the female portion of the population, we can increase the numbers of these organizations to show our elected officials how important their support is to this global crisis.

It is also important to keep track of what your representatives are doing once they're in office. Very few people ever take this responsibility. Call your representatives' offices every six months and ask them for copies of their voting records. Environmental organizations also track the voting records of elected officials and have this information available.

Keep writing to your representatives (remember the suggestion to keep prestamped postcards on hand?) and let them know how you want them to vote. Write, "I am a member of your congressional district, and I want you to vote for saving the environment and endangered species." Letters and postcards are given more credence, but if you haven't the time, then telephone or e-mail.

Become part of a larger group of individuals who have joined together to increase their power and effectiveness. For example, the Sierra Club is one of the oldest and best known organizations, with satellite groups in almost every city. Its victories on behalf of the environment include saving Alaska's Admiralty Island from the logging companies. The Sierra Club Legal Defense Fund has also forced Union Oil Company to clean up refinery wastewater in the San Francisco Bay. They stopped the oil industry from exploding 10,000 dynamite charges in Florida's Big Cypress National Preserve, one of the richest wildlife areas.

Greenpeace, another environmental group, is working to save the Arctic and Antarctica from irresponsible drilling and oil exploration by Arco and British Petroleum. They are also working in many ways to stop global warming.

The World Wildlife Fund Living Planet campaign is saving endangered species and animals who live all over the globe, from the Florida panther, one of the most endangered species in the United States, to the hawkfill turtles of the Menai Bay Marine Ecosystem in East Africa.

These are only three of the many active groups that depend on our interests and passions. If you love birds, join the Audubon Society; if you love wildlife, join the Defenders of Wildlife or the Wildlife Society. Help preserve the land and habitat by joining the Nature Conservancy. If you love the oceans, join the Jacques Cousteau Society or Save Our Shores. There is a partial list in the Resources section at the back of the book. Research others. Your membership and support of these groups is of utmost importance at this time.

Do something each week and see how empowered it makes you feel. When we feel helpless, it's often because we aren't helping. We need to promote and support what we believe in to give our lives meaning and to feel our power. Enough of this public apathy! Don't expect someone else to act on your behalf. Do something yourself! Remember the 1,600 scientists who warned us that we only have a short time to turn the tide before it's too late. In our minds, in our hearts, in our wombs, we know that *now is the time for us to make a difference!*

A New Spiritual Global Consciousness

Mother Earth speaks to us softly with the gentle babble of a stream, the harmonious sounds of the ocean waves. She heals our human energy with the soft rustling sound of the wind in the trees and the sweet song of birds. She provides warmth, water, shelter, and food. As women, we share our understanding that the Earth is a living organism that sustains us. If we don't sustain her, we will not survive. We must plan and act for the generations to come after us if they are to survive, as well.

Women have the opportunity to lead a grand awakening of the spirit and to transform the collective unconscious. Our values in economic and political arenas have to change because they are so out of synch with the reality of our worldwide environmental crisis.

The Elders say that everything in the universe knows of its harmony, balance, alignment, and connection with all other things, except humans. The spiritual solution is that we can learn to be enlightened enough to see how we are connected to all things and that together we make the whole that is Mother Earth. Once we feel this connection, how can we plunder, kill, or rape her?

Let us honor her cycles and those of nature and sacred law. Let us respect other species and nurture their sacredness as the Great Spirit's children and as our brothers and sisters. In this way we can change our spiritual perceptions. We can utilize our technologies in this ecological movement. We can create other solutions rather than using up nonrenewable resources. We can live within the budget of resources Mother Earth gives us. We can reduce our materialistic desires and recommit to simpler lifestyles of moderation.

Awakening to our own spirit and power as women illuminates for us our intimate spiritual connections. We are energy beings of light and dark. It is our choice where we focus our intent and our energies.

It is said that one person alone can move a pebble; that many people together can move a mountain. And even though there may be thousands of people involved, ultimately it is the additional effort of *just one more* person that tips the scales and makes the difference! Each of us must act as though we are that person, as though our one additional action is the one that will cause the radical paradigm shift and the breakthrough.

We can do it. We must do it. *Now* is truly our time.

To recapture the important points of this chapter:

1. Despite the dire news about the problems facing our planet, we have cause for hope. Nature is the greatest healer, and we can learn from her how to rebalance the feminine and masculine energies.

2. Connect with a tree or another plant. Let its energy sustain you. Practice the Tree Meditation often, perhaps on a daily basis.

3. Envision women joining together by the millions and hundreds of millions, each doing at least one small act of power a week to help save life on planet Earth.

4. Educate yourself and take action to restore the environment. Do something! Now!

Epilogue:
Now It's Our Turn

*When women can take their power through
the heart of the masculine and when men can
come to problems through the heart of the
feminine, the world will be peaceful.*

THE ELDERS

I have presented the facts to you—the research on women's personal life, and about women's work in the home and in the world. I have presented facts concerning the realities of other women around the planet. And I have illustrated the fact that the Earth is dying unless we take action now.

As I sit here on the very eve of the destruction of Mother Earth, I wonder whether we will go numb with denial, as we have done so often in the past. For hundreds of years our denial has kept us as victims in families that were molesting and abusing us, in jobs that were underpaying us, with governments that wouldn't acknowledge us, and in a world that is being destroyed around us. Will we once again enter into that dark denial, hoping, as usual, for men to save us?

It is time for us to take our personal power. When will we decide to change? When will we take responsibility, respond with the ability to change the present crisis, and balance the energies of the male and the female? Does more destruction have to happen for us to wake up? We have buried our heads in the sand for so long. Will we continue to do so?

The time to act is now. There are many things you can do — many acts of power. You can take power in your relationships with integrity and dignity. You can take your power in the workplace and beyond to effect change in our governments and world structures so that decisions will be made for healing and harmony rather than for weapons, war, and ecological destruction. You can see to it that strong feminine energy balances the decisions men are making. You can also see to it that other women — your sisters — have a chance in life for education, self-sufficiency, autonomy, peace, and health. And you can see to it that your mother, the Earth, is able to continue a long and productive and nurturing life, not only for human beings, but for animals and plants, for this matrix that is the living Earth — Mother Earth — Gaia.

What more can you ask than to be reawakened, than to be a part of this great reestablishment of a true balance of power? This can be a time of magic, a time when women come together — all ethnicities, races, nationalities, and sexual orientations. It's time for us to risk pushing our edge for change by valuing one another as women and trusting in the power of feminine energy as absolutely necessary for true change to occur. If you only take one suggestion from this book, take it and *live* it. Take it out into the world, and go with power. Make a difference. Make a difference for yourself, for your children, for children yet unborn, and for the world. The resurgence of feminine energy will balance the masculine energy and shift the collective unconscious. One action, just one act of power by each of us, and together we can change the world.

Now it's our turn!

Our worst fear is not that we are inadequate,
our deepest fear is that we are powerful beyond measure.
It is our light, not our darkness that most frightens us.
We ask ourselves, "Who am I to be brilliant, gorgeous,
talented and fabulous?"
Actually, who are you not to be?
You are a child of God; your playing small
doesn't serve the world.
There is nothing enlightened about shrinking
so that other people won't feel insecure around you.
We were born to make manifest the glory of God within us.
It is not just in some of us, it is in everyone,
and as we let our own light shine
we unconsciously give other people permission to do the same.
As we are liberated from our own fear,
our presence automatically liberates others.

NELSON MANDELA

Resources

Women's Resources

American Association of University Women
1111 16th St. NW
Washington, DC 20036
202-785-7712
Supports and promotes educational equality for women and girls.

American Civil Liberties Union, Women's Project
132 W. 43rd St.
New York, NY 10036
212-944-9800
Seeks constitutional equality through litigation.

American Women's Economic Development Corporation
71 Vanderbilt Ave.
New York, NY 10169
212-688-1900
Supports women's economic equality.

Amnesty International USA, Women and Human Rights Project
322 8th Ave.
New York, NY 10001
212-633-4200
Public education to empower people to act to eliminate human rights abuses against women internationally.

EMILY's List
805 15th St. NW, Ste. 400
Washington, DC 20005
Helps female candidates with financial funds for elections and education on campaigning.

The Fund for the Feminist Majority
1600 Wilson Blvd., Ste. 704
Arlington, VA 22209
703-522-2214
Works for women's rights and abortion rights.

International Women's Rights Action Watch
Humphrey Institute of Public Affairs
University of Minnesota
301 19th Ave. South
Minneapolis, MN 55455
Publishes the Women's Watch Newsletter — International Women's Rights Action Watch.

League of Women Voters
1730 M St. NW, Ste. 1000
Washington, DC 20036
202-429-1965
Works to encourage and educate women and others in the governmental and political process.

National Abortion Rights League
1156 15th St. NW, Ste. 700
Washington, DC 20005
202-828-9300
Pro-choice group.

National Coalition Against Domestic Violence
P.O. Box 34103
Washington, DC 20043
202-638-6388
Works to end domestic violence.

National Organization of Women (NOW)
1000 16th St. NW, Ste. 700
Washington, DC 10036
202-331-0066
Organization devoted to women achieving equality.

National Women's Party
144 Constitution Ave. NE
Washington, DC 20036
202-546-1210
Supports and works for the passage in Congress of the Equal Rights Amendment.

9 to 5 Association of Working Women
238 W. Wisconsin Ave.
Milwaukee, WI 53202
414-274-0925
Helps working women with work-related issues of harassment, discrimination, and so on.

Older Women's League
666 11th St. NW
Washington, DC 20001
202-783-6686
Supports issues concerning midlife and older women.

U.S. Network for Women
633 Pennsylvania Ave. NW
Washington, DC 20004
202-737-0120
An expanded network of organizations and individuals who support women's economic, political, and social empowerment worldwide.

Women's Environment & Development Organization
355 Lexington Ave., 3rd Floor
New York, NY 10017
212-973-0325
Works on behalf of environmental and economic development issues.

Environmental Groups

Many of these addresses and phone numbers are for Washington, D.C., but if you contact their national headquarters, they can also give you the number for the office or group in your area.

American Forestry Association
1516 P Street NW
Washington, DC 20005
202-667-3300
National citizens' organization for reforesting.

American Rivers
801 Pennsylvania Ave. SE
Washington, DC 20003
202-547-6900
Nationwide organization for preserving the nation's rivers and ecosystems.

Center for Marine Conservation
1235 DeSales St. NW
Washington, DC 20036
202-429-5609
National organization dedicated to protecting marine wildlife and its habitat.

Co-Op America
1612 K St. NW, Ste. 600
Washington, DC 20077
202-872-5307
This group publishes the National Green Pages, *which we should all have on hand. They list 100 categories of products, services, and companies which are environmentally responsible.*

The Cousteau Society
930 W. 21st St.
Norfolk, VA 23517
(804) 627-1144
An international nonprofit organization dedicated to the protection and improvement of the quality of life of future generations.

Defenders of Wildlife
1244 19th St. NW
Washington, DC 20036
202-659-9510
National nonprofit that protects wild animals in their natural settings.

Environmental Defense Fund
257 Park Ave. South
New York, NY 10010
212-505-2100
EDF is one of the oldest environmental action organizations.

Greenpeace, USA
1436 U Street
Washington, DC 20009
202-462-1177
International environmental organization protecting and preserving the natural world, working on toxic pollution, ocean ecology, nuclear issues, and atmospheric issues.

League of Conservation Voters
1150 Connecticut Ave. NW, Suite 201
Washington, DC 20036
202-785-8683
This organization is dedicated to the election of pro-environmentalist candidates to Congress. They support candidates who take a strong stand against polluters.

National Audubon Society
950 Third Ave.
New York, NY 10022
212-832-3200
They are the oldest conservation group focusing on conserving native wildlife and habitat.

National Resources Defense Council
40 West 20th St.
New York, NY 10011
212-727-2700
Dedicated to protecting the natural environment and improving the quality of the human environment.

National Wildlife Federation
1412 16th St. NW
Washington, DC 20036
202-797-6800
The largest environmental group, NFW focuses on the protection of the global environment and wildlife.

Nature Conservancy
1815 N. Lynn St.
Arlington, VA 22209
1-800-628-6860
Works to preserve the Earth's rare plants, animals, and natural environments.

Pacific Whale Foundation
101 North Kihei Rd.
Kihei, Maui, HI 96753
1-800-942-5311
Works for preservation of the marine environment and the Adopt-a-Whale program.

Sierra Club
730 Polk St.
San Francisco, CA 94109
415-776-2211
*This organization was established in 1892 and continues to work
to protect the environment on many levels. There are many local
chapters throughout the U.S.*

20/20 Vision
1828 Jefferson Pl. NW
Washington, DC 20077-6582
202-833-2020
*This unique organization keeps its eyes and ears on congressional
representatives and their bills and keeps you alerted to the bills you
need to follow up on by writing your representatives. They ask for
twenty minutes of your time each month to promote protection
of the environment and peace.*

Union of Concerned Scientists
Two Battle Square
Cambridge, MA 02238-9105
617-547-5552
*This nonprofit organization is dedicated to advancing responsible
public policies in areas where science and technology play a critical
role. They have an action alert program to keep you informed on congressional progress or tactics so you can write to your representatives.*

World Watch Institute
1776 Massachusetts Ave. NW
Washington, DC 20036
202-452-1999
This group publishes one of the most crucial books every year, entitled
State of the World. *They are a nonprofit, nonpartisan research organization and think tank that makes available their global information
on the environment.*

World Wildlife Fund
1250 24th St. NW
Washington, DC 20037
202-293-4800
They help protect the world's creatures and habitat. They are committed to preserving the abundance and diversity of life on Earth, balancing human needs with nature.

Responsible Investment Opportunities

The following organizations offer ways to invest your money with a social conscience. Please consider exploring these options with your financial adviser.

Citizens' Trust
Citizens Index Fund
1 Harbor Place
Portsmouth, NH 03801
1-800-223-7010
Manages five funds, all socially responsible.

Domini Social Equity Fund
11 West 25th, 7th Floor
New York, NY 10010-2001
1-800-762-6814
Amy Domini is a national figure in social investing; includes Equity and Index Fund comprised of 400 companies that have been socially screened.

Green Money Journal
608 West Glass Avenue
Spokane, WA 99205
1-800-318-5725
Lists and tracks fifty mutual funds; first-class quarterly publication.

Resourceful Women
P.O. Box 29423
San Francisco, CA 94129
415-561-6520
A nonprofit member organization that helps to educate women with at least $50,000 to invest.

Women's Equity Fund
P.O. Box 856
Cincinnati, OH 45264-0856
1-800-385-7003
Pro-conscience Women's Equity Fund founded by Linda Pei.

Notes

Chapter 1

1. Barbara Walker, *The Woman's Encyclopedia of Myths and Secrets* (New York: Harper & Row, 1983), p. 266.
2. James Lovelock, *The Ages of Gaia: A Biography of Our Living Earth* (New York: W. W. Norton, 1988).
3. Lester Brown, Christopher Flavin, and Sandra Postel, *Saving the Planet* (New York: W. W. Norton, 1991), p. 20.
4. Paula DiPerna, "Truth vs. Facts," *Ms. Magazine,* vol. II, no. 2, p. 22.
5. Will Steger and Jon Bowermaster, *Saving the Earth* (New York: Alfred Knopf, 1990), p. 31.
6. William K. Stevens, "New Evidence Finds This Is the Warmest Century in 600 Years," *New York Times,* April 28, 1998; see also Brown, Flavin, and Postel, *Saving the Planet,* p. 28.
7. Eugene Linden, *Time,* March 1994, p. 79.
8. Brown, Flavin, and Postel, *State of the World, 1994* (New York: W. W. Norton, 1994), p. 19.

Chapter 2

1. Georgia Witkin, "Quick Fixes and Small Comforts," *Self Magazine,* July 1989, p. 117.
2. Shere Hite, *Women and Love* (New York: St. Martin's Press, 1987), p. 27.
3. Jessie Bernard, *The Future of Marriage* (New Haven, CT: Yale Univ. Press, 1982), pp. 26-27.
4. "Gender Influences Marital Dissatisfaction and Divorce," *Menninger Letter,* vol 4, no. 1, Jan. 1996, p. 1.

Chapter 3

1. Franklin Thesaurus Wordmaster.
2. Lederer and Jackson, *The Mirages of Marriage* (New York: W. W. Norton, 1968), p. 53.
3. Ibid.
4. Franklin Thesaurus Wordmaster.
5. Deborah Tannen, *You Just Don't Understand* (New York: Ballantine, 1990).
6. Kaichi Tohei, *Ki in Daily Life* (New York: Wehman Brothers, 1978), p. 95.

Chapter 4

1. Shere Hite, *Hite Report on Female Sexuality* (New York: Dell, 1976), p. 229.
2. William H. Masters and Virginia E. Johnson, *Human Sexual Response* (Boston: Little Brown, 1966).
3. Ibid.

Chapter 5

1. William H. Masters and Virginia E. Johnson, *Human Sexual Response* (Boston: Little, Brown, 1966).
2. Ibid.
3. Margaret Andersen, *Thinking About Women* (New York: Macmillan, 1992), p. 225.
4. Merlin Stone, *When God Was a Woman* (San Diego, CA: Harcourt, Brace, Jovanovich, 1976), p. 222.
5. SwiftDeer, American Indian Teachings, oral tradition.

Chapter 6

1. McGoldrick, Anderson, and Walsh, *Women in Families* (New York: W. W. Norton, 1989), p. 273. See also Judith Lorber, *Paradoxes of Gender* (New Haven, CT: Yale Univ. Press, 1994), p. 213.
2. Margaret Andersen, *Thinking About Women* (New York: Macmillan, 1992), p. 146.

3. McGoldrick et al., *Women in Families,* p. 209.
4. Stallard, Ehrenreich, and Saylar, *Poverty in the American Dream* (Boston: South End Press, 1983), p. 12.
5. Andersen, *Thinking About Women,* p. 139.
6. McGoldrick et al., *Women in Families,* p. 209.
7. Andersen, *Thinking About Women,* p. 161. See also Susan May, "Home Sweet Work," in *California Monthly,* September 1997, pp. 22-25.
8. McGoldrick et al., *Women in Families,* p. 271.
9. Ibid., p. 369.
10. Andersen, *Thinking About Women,* p. 161.
11. Sara Rex, ed., *The American Woman 1990–1991* (New York: W. W. Norton, 1991), p. 13.
12. David Blankenhorn, *Fatherless in America* (New York: HarperCollins, 1995), pp. 130, 132.
13. Gilda Berger, *Women, Work, and Wages* (New York: Franklin Watts, 1986), p. 15.
14. Adam Clymer, "Child-Support Net Usually Fails," *New York Times,* July 17, 1997, p. A16.
15. U.S. Department of Labor, *Women's Bureau Facts on Working Women* no. 93-2, June (Washington, DC: Government Printing Office, 1993). See also Diana M. Pearce, "Something Old, Something New: Women's Poverty in the 1990s," in Sherri Matteo, ed., *American Women in the Nineties: Today's Critical Issues* (Boston: Northeastern Univ. Press, 1993), pp. 79-97.
16. "Women Through the Family Life Cycle," McGoldrick; Hoffman, 1972, 1974; Lasoff, 1974; Padan, 1965.
17. Andersen, *Thinking About Women,* pp. 161, 182.

Chapter 7

1. John Kenneth Galbraith, *Economics and Public Purpose* (San Diego, CA: Houghton Mifflin, 1973).
2. Charlotte O'Kelly and Larry Carney, *Women and Men in Society,* 2nd ed. (Belmont, CA: Wadsworth, 1986), p. 123.
3. Hilkka Pietila and Jeanne Vickers, *Making Women Matter: The Role of the United Nations* (New York: Zed Books, 1994), p. 131.

4. Marilyn French, *The War Against Women* (New York: Summit Books, 1992), p. 35.
5. Judith Lorber, *Paradoxes of Gender* (New Haven, CT: Yale Univ. Press, 1994), p. 288.
6. Marilyn Waring, *If Women Counted* (San Francisco: Harper & Row, 1988).
7. O'Kelly and Csrney, *Women and Men in Society*, p. 123.
8. H. Pietila and J. Vickers, eds., *Making Women Matter: The Role of the United Nations* (London: Zed Books, 1994), p. 131.
9. Margaret Andersen, *Thinking About Women* (New York: Macmillan, 1992), p. 143.
10. Ibid.
11. Gilda Berger, *Women, Work and Wages* (New York: Franklin Watts, 1986), p. 3.
12. Deborah Tannen, *You Just Don't Understand* (New York: Ballantine, 1990), p. 31.
13. Janet Shibley Hyde, *Half the Human Experience* (Lexington, MA: D. C. Heath, 1985), p. 85.
14. Vernon Howard, *Your Power to Say NO* (New York: New Life Foundation, 1981), pp. 13, 18.
15. Linda Ellerbee, *Move On: Adventures in the Real World* (New York: G. P. Putnam's Sons, 1991).

Chapter 8

1. "Sentiment and Women's Roles," *Los Angeles Times*, Sept. 15, 1981.
2. Ibid.
3. Cited in article by Maggie Scarf, *Lear's* magazine, June 1989, p. 73.
4. U.S. Dept. of Labor, *Women's Bureau Facts on Working Women*, no. 96-2, Sept. (Washington, DC: Goverment Printing Office, 1996).
5. "Why Women Still Don't Hit the Top," *Fortune*, July 30, 1990. For an overview of women's inequality in the work force, see Judith Lorber, *Paradoxes of Gender* (New Haven, CT: Yale Univ. Press, 1994), pp. 194-222.
6. U.S. Dept. of Labor, *Women's Bureau Facts on Working Women: Women in Management*, no. 97-3, April (Washington, DC: Government Printing Office, 1997).
7. The Feminist Majority Letter, 1994.

8. U.S. Dept. of Labor, *Women's Bureau Facts on Working Women: Women in Management,* no. 97-3, April (Washington, DC: Government Printing Office, 1997).
9. Holly Hale, "A Woman's Place," *Psychology Today,* Apr. 1988.
10. *Los Angeles Times,* June 9, 1991.
11. The Feminist Majority Letter, 1994.
12. U.S. Dept. of Labor, *Women's Bureau Facts on Working Women: 20 Facts on Women Workers,* no. 96-2, Sept. (Washington, DC: Government Printing Office, 1996).
13. *Psychology Today* magazine, April 1988, p. 28.
14. U.S. Bureau of the Census, *Statistical Abstract,* 116th edition (Washington, DC: Government Printing Office, 1996).
15. Susan Faludi, *Backlash* (New York, Crown, 1991), p. 365.
16. U.S. Bureau of Labor Statistics, 1996.
17. U.S. Report to the United Nations on the Status of Women, 1985–1994, p. 64.
18. Julianne Malveaux, "On the Economy: Differing Views of Women's Status," *San Francisco Examiner,* Jul. 6, 1997, p. D-2. See also "Continuing Struggle for Women's Equality," *Now Times,* May-June 1991, p. 15.
19. *Cosmopolitan* magazine, Feb. 1991.
20. "Equal Pay Top Issue for Women: One-Third of Female Workers Polled Say They're Shortchanged," *New York Times,* Sept. 5, 1997.
21. "SEC Weighs In Again on Issue of Executive Pay," *Los Angeles Times,* May 11, 1992.
22. Judith H. Doborzynski, "Growing Trend: Giant Payoffs for Executives Who Fail Big," *New York Times,* July 21, 1997, p. D1.
23. John Leo, "When 20 Million Isn't Enough," *U.S. News and World Report,* Oct. 9, 1995, p. 26.
24. U.S. Bureau of the Census, *Statistical Abstract,* 116th edition (Washington, DC: Government Printing Office, 1996).
25. U.S. Dept. of Labor, *Women's Bureau Facts on Working Women: 20 Facts on Women Workers,* no. 96-2, Sept. (Washington, DC: Government Printing Office, 1996). For more on women's poverty, see Diana M. Pearce, "Something Old, Something New: Women's Poverty in the 1990s," in Sherri Matteo, ed., *American Women in the Nineties: Today's Critical Issues* (Boston: Northeastern Univ. Press, 1993) pp. 79-97.

26. "Dead Beat Dads," *Newsweek,* May 4, 1992.
27. U.S. Bureau of the Census, *Statistical Abstract,* 116th edition (Washington, DC: Government Printing Office, 1996).
28. Ibid.
29. Older Women's League, *The Path to Poverty: An Analysis of Women's Retirement Income,* May 1997 (Washington, DC: Older Women's League, 1997).
30. L. W. Hewlett, *Modern Maturity* magazine, April-May 1992, p. 82.
31. U.S. Bureau of the Census, *Statistical Abstract,* 116th edition (Washington, DC: Government Printing Office, 1996). See also American Association of Retired Persons, *Bulletin,* June 1992, vol. 33, no. 6.

Chapter 9

1. Jean Baker-Miller, *Toward a New Psychology of Women* (Boston: Beacon Press, 1986).
2. Peter T. Kilburn, "Women and Minorities Still Face Glass Ceiling, Study Says," *New York Times,* Mar. 16, 1995.
3. Jean Baker-Miller, *Toward a New Psychology of Women,* chapter 1.
4. Cited in Cynthia Fuchs Epstein, *Deceptive Distinctions* (New Haven, CT: Yale Univ. Press, 1988).
5. Alfred Adler, cited in Henri Ellenberger, *The Discovery of the Unconscious* (New York: Basic Books, 1981), p. 223.
6. Epstein, *Deceptive Distinctions,* p. 9.
7. *EuroBusiness* magazine, Dec. 1994, p. 7.

Chapter 10

1. "Perspective on the Sexes," *Los Angeles Times,* Feb. 20, 1992.
2. American Psychiatric Association, *Diagnostic and Statistical Manual of Mental Disorders III-R* (Washington, DC: American Psychiatric Association, 1987), p. 353.
3. Gail L. Zellman, *Women and Sex Roles, Politics and Power* (Boston: Houghton Mifflin, 1978), p. 346.
4. Jean Shinoda Bolen, *Ring of Power* (San Francisco: Harper-SanFrancisco, 1993), p. 201.
5. Ibid.

6. Jean Baker-Miller, *Toward a New Psychology of Women* (Boston: Beacon Press, 1986), p. 117.
7. Harley SwiftDeer Reagan, Deertribe, Rainbow Powers Center.
8. Franklin Thesaurus Wordmaster.
9. *Judy Lee Program,* Business Radio Network, July 11, 1992.
10. Deborah Tannen, *You Just Don't Understand* (New York: Ballantine, 1990), p. 75.
11. Tannen, *You Just Don't Understand,* pp. 302-15.
12. Baker-Miller, *Toward a New Psychology of Women,* p. 10.

Chapter 11

1. Patricia Aburdene and John Naisbitt, *Megatrends for Women* (New York: Fawcett, 1993), p. 76.
2. Juliet Nierenberg and Irene S. Ross, *Women and the Art of Negotiating* (New York: Simon & Schuster, 1985).
3. Phyllis Katz, Ph.D., and Margaret Katz, *The Feminist Dollar: The Wise Women's Buying Guide* (New York: Plenum, 1997).
4. Letha Dawson Scanzoni and John Scanzoni, Men, *Women and Change* (New York: McGraw-Hill, 1981), p. 48.
5. Ibid., p. 48.
6. Aburdene and Naisbitt, *Megatrends for Women,* pp. 62-63.
7. National Association of Women's Business Owners, *Success Magazine,* Dec. 1995.

Chapter 12

1. June Sochen, *Her Story* (Palo Alto, CA: Mayfield Publishing, 1982), pp. 249, 304.
2. Ibid., p. 62.
3. National Women's Political Caucus, "Fact Sheets on Women's Political Progress," June 1997.
4. Anne Wilson Schaef, *Women's Realities* (Minneapolis: Winston Press, 1981), p. 2.
5. See, for example, Linda Bird Francke, *Ground Zero: The Gender Wars in the Military* (New York: Simon & Schuster, 1997), and Eric Schmitt, "Army Inquiries Find a Wide Bias Against Women," *New York Times,* July 31, 1997, p. A1.

6. June Sochen, *Her Story,* p. 125.
7. Ruth Leger Sivard, *World Military and Social Expenditures 1996* (Washington, DC: World Priorities, 1996).
8. Information from War Resisters League, New York City, 1997.
9. Sivard, *World Military and Social Expenditures 1996,* p. 41.
10. Marilyn Waring, *If Women Counted* (San Francisco: Harper & Row, 1988), pp. 168, 170.
11. Sivard, *World Military and Social Expenditures 1996,* p. 11.
12. Ibid., pp. 5, 11.
13. Waring, *If Women Counted,* p. 169.
14. Toni Seager and Ann Olson, *Women in the World* (New York: Simon & Schuster/Touchstone Books, 1986), p. 115. See also Ruth Leger Sivard, *Women: A World Survey* (Washington, DC: World Priorities, 1987), p. 38, for the same point about women worldwide.
15. Stephen Hawking, *Black Holes and Baby Universes* (New York: Bantam Doubleday/Dell Audio Publishing, 1993), tape 3, side 6.
16. Marilyn French, *The War Against Women* (New York: Summit Books, 1992), p. 35.
17. National Women's Political Caucus, "Fact Sheet on Women's Political Progress," June 1997.
18. Pearl S. Buck, "Women's Roles," *Harper's Bazaar,* 1938.

Chapter 13

1. "The War Against Women," *U.S. News & World Report,* Mar. 28, 1994.
2. "India: Till Death Do Us Part," *Time,* Special Issue, Fall 1990, p. 39.
3. John F. Burns, "India's Five Decades of Progress and Pain," *New York Times,* Aug. 14, 1997, p. A11.
4. University of Minnesota, *The Women's Watch,* Sept. 1994.
5. *Feminist Majority Report,* Summer 1994, p. 13.
6. Toni Seager, *The State of Women in the World Atlas* (New York, Penguin, 1997), p. 27.
7. "Life Behind the Veil," *Time,* Special Issue, Fall 1990, p. 37.
8. Ruth Leger Sivard, *Women: A World Survey* (Washington, DC: World Priorities, 1987), pp. 32-33.
9. Toni Seager and Ann Olson, *Women in the World* (New York: Simon & Schuster/Touchstone Books, 1986), p. 102.

10. *U.S. News & World Report,* Mar. 28, 1994.
11. Harry Lightfoot-Klein, *Prisoners of Ritual* (New York: Harrington Park Press, 1989).
12. *National Now Times,* Nov.-Dec. 1990, p. 18.
13. "Asia: Discarding Daughters," *Time,* Special Issue, Fall 1990, p. 40.
14. Toni Seager, *The State of Women in the World Atlas,* p. 34.
15. Ibid.
16. Marilyn French, *The War Against Women* (New York: Summit Books, 1992), p. 105.
17. Jodi L. Jacobson, "Gender Bias: Roadblock to Sustainable Development" World Institute, paper 110, 1992, p. 15.
18. Ruth Leger Sivard, *Women: A World Survey,* rev. ed. (Washington, DC: World Priorities, 1995), p. 27.
19. *National Now Times,* May-June 1991, p. 11.
20. Seager and Olson, *Women: A World Survey,* p. 104.
21. French, *The War Against Women,* p. 105.
22. Anna H. Phelan, "The Latest Political Weapon in Haiti: Mililary Rapes of Women and Girls," *Los Angeles Times,* June 5, 1994.
23. Donatella Lorch, "Wave of Rape Adds New Horror to Rwanda's Trail of Brutality," *New York Times,* May 15, 1995.
24. Hubert Humphrey Institute of Public Affairs, University of Minnesota, *The Women's Watch,* June 1995, pp. 3-4.
25. Ibid.
26. "The War Against Women," *U.S. News & World Report,* Mar. 28, 1994.
27. *New Woman Spirit,* Winter 1990.

Chapter 14

1. Ann Campbell, *The Opposite Sex* (Topsfield, MA: Salem House, 1989), pp. 64, 172.
2. *Women's Environmental and Development Organization Newsletter,* vol. 9, no. 3–4, Nov.–Dec. 1997.
3. *Connections Newsletter,* vol. 1, no. 1, Mar. 1995, p. 3.
4. Hilkka Pietila and Jeanne Vickers, *Making Women Matter: The Role of the United Nations* (London: Zed Books, 1994), pp. 147-54.
5. Katarina Tomasevski, *Women and Human Rights* (London: Zed Books, 1993), p. 117.

6. Rogin Morgan, ed., *Sisterhood Is Global* (New York: Anchor Books/
   Doubleday, 1984), p. 471.
7. Marilyn French, *The War Against Women* (New York: Summit
   Books, 1993), p. 204.
8. Christine Onyango, *Feminist Majority Newsletter,* Winter 1995, p. 9.
9. Hubert Humphrey Institute of Public Affairs, University of
   Minnesota, *The Women's Watch,* Sept. 1994.
10. There are many women's organizations and NGOs that financially
    sponsor individuals to attend the U.N. Conference on Women. For
    further information about guidelines and applications, contact your
    local women's organization.
11. Morgan, ed., *Sisterhood Is Global,* p. 493.

Chapter 15

1. Quoted in David Suzuki and Peter Knudtson, *Wisdom of the Elders:
   Sacred Native Stories of Nature* (New York: Bantam, 1992), p. 236.
2. Quoted in Suzuki and Knudtson, *Wisdom of the Elders,* pp. 233–34.
3. Bob Drogin, *Los Angeles Times,* Oct. 14, 1995.
4. Glen Reynolds and Robert Merges, *Outer Space: Problems of Law
   and Policy* (Boulder, CO: Westview Pres, 1989), p. 12.
5. Martyn Bramwell, *Book of Planet Earth* (New York: Simon &
   Schuster, 1992), p. 169.
6. "Global Climate Data Show Return of Warming Trend," *EDF Letter,*
   vol. 26, no. 3, May 1995.
7. Ross Gelbspan, *The Heat Is On* (New York: Addison-Wesley, 1997),
   p. 150.
8. Ibid, p. 148.
9. Elliot Diringer, "Island Nations Feel Water Rising: Leaders Ask
   Industrial Countries to Curb Global Warming," *San Francisco
   Chronicle,* June 25, 1997, p. A-2.
10. Lester Brown, Christopher Flavin, Hilary French, *State of the World
    1997* (New York: Norton, 1997), pp. 78–79.
11. Will Steger and Jon Bowermaster, *Saving the Planet* (New York:
    Alfred Knopf, 1990), p. 31.
12. Alan Weisman, "The Naked Planet," *Los Angeles Times Magazine,*
    Apr. 5, 1992.

13. Ibid.
14. Al Gore, *Earth in the Balance* (Boston: Houghton Mifflin, 1992), p. 84.
15. World Resources Institute, *Environmental Almanac* (Boston: Houghton Mifflin, 1992), p. 146.
16. World Watch Institute, *Vital Signs* (New York: W. W. Norton, 1995), pp. 116, 119.
17. Roger DiSilvestro, *The Endangered Species* (New York: John Wiley & sons, 1989), p. 220.
18. Steger and Bowermaster, *Saving the Planet,* p. 93.
19. David Malin Roodman, "Carbon Emissions Resume Rise," in Lester Brown, Lenseen, and Kane, eds., *Vital Signs 1995* (New York: W. W. Norton, 1995), p. 66.
20. World Resources Institute, *Environmental Almanac,* p. 143.
21. Ibid.
22. Steven Hackin, *Global Renaissance* (Los Angeles: Globe Press, 1991), p. 31.
23. Natural Resources Defense Council.
24. Roger DiSilvestro, *The Endangered Kingdom* (New York: Wiley Science Editions, 1989), p. 38.
25. Richard Preston, *The Hot Zone* (New York: Anchor Books, 1995), p. 4.
26. Ibid., p. 16.
27. Alan Ereika, *The Elder Brothers* (New York: Vintage Books, 1993), p. 225.
28. Helen Caldicott, *If You Love This Planet* (New York: W. W. Norton, 1992), p. 75.
29. Al Gore, *Earth in the Balance,* p. 109.
30. Richard Barnet and John Cavanaugh, *Global Dreams: Imperial Corporations and the New World Order* (New York: Touchstone, Simon and Schuster, 1994), p. 255.
31. Jane Ellen Stevens, "New Project Investigates Mystery Deaths and Illnesses," *New York Times,* Mar. 25, 1997.
32. Julie Califano, "A Clear Look at Water Purity," *Food & Wine* magazine, Nov. 1995, pp. 130, 132.
33. Timothy White, "Pray for the Water, Pray for the Land," *Shaman's Drum* magazine, no. 38, 1995, p. 33.
34. Steger and Bowermaster, *Saving the Planet,* p. 168.

35. Jay Grimes, Professor of Microbiology, Statement to California Coastal Commission, June 13, 1990.
36. Environmental Defense Fund, *30th Annual Report,* 1967–1997, p. 11.
37. Caldicott, *If You Love This Planet,* pp. 86-87.
38. World Resources Institute, *Environmental Almanac,* pp. 136-37.
39. David Suzuki and Peter Knudtson, *Wisdom of the Elders* (New York: Bantam, 1992), p. 110.
40. Alan Weisman, "The Naked Planet."
41. Marla Cone, "Sexual Confusion in the Wild," *Los Angeles Times,* Oct. 2, 1994.
42. Reported in the Proceedings of the National Academy of Sciences, as noted on Ozone Action Website News, Mar. 1, 1998.
43. World Watch Institute, *State of the World 1995,* p. 4.
44. Bramwell, *Book of Planet Earth,* p. 177.
45. Jared Diamond, *The Third Chimpanzee* (San Francisco: Harper Perennials, 1993), p. 360.
46. Ibid.
47. Steve Levin, Science Section, *Spirit* magazine, Nov. 1995, p. 94.

Chapter 16

1. *Los Angeles Times,* Sept. 21. 1997, p. A-23.
2. *Los Angeles Times,* Feb. 28, 1998, p. A-18.

Index